GLENCOE

VOCABULARY BUILDER

Peter Fischer, Editorial Consultant

National-Louis University

Course 7

 **Glencoe**

New York, New York   Columbus, Ohio   Chicago, Illinois   Peoria, Illinois   Woodland Hills, California

Acknowledgments
The pronunciation key used in the glossary has been reproduced by permission
from *The American Heritage Dictionary of the English Language, Fourth Edition.*
Copyright © 2000 by Houghton Mifflin Company.

 **Glencoe**

The **McGraw·Hill** Companies

Printed in the United States of America

Send all inquiries to:
Glencoe/McGraw-Hill
8787 Orion Place
Columbus, OH 43240

SE ISBN: 0-07-861672-7
ATE ISBN: 0-07-861673-5

5 6 7 8 9 10 113 10 09

Contents

Name _____

Art at the Threshold

Regardless of the culture, home is where the spirit of a people is **palpable**. In India, the home is almost **sacrosanct**, a reflection of one's innermost person. On earthen surfaces in their native country and on the concrete doorsteps of homes in their adopted nations, Indian women carry out the
5 ancient tradition of *rangoli,* decorating the threshold with turmeric, indigo, lentils, and other natural substances. These designs provide a vibrant welcome mat to even the most **modest** dwelling.

The exact origins of *rangoli* are unknown, but art historians assume that the tradition began as a form of thanksgiving. To the people of India, the
10 floor is synonymous with the earth, a mother figure that supports all life. To **adorn** the floor of a house is to honor the house and the earth as special places. The art form has an added dimension, teaching children that beauty in the home is something that can be created easily and does not require material possessions.

15 While *rangoli* designs vary from region to region and family to family, they follow **prescriptive** patterns, often a series of dots or dashes aligned in the shapes of plants, animals, gods and goddesses, or geometric forms. Although thin sticks wound with cloth are sometimes used, the basic tool for *rangoli* is the hand. The artist begins by placing her materials in small
20 containers with wide brims. After selecting a freshly swept spot on the floor or doorstep, she creates her designs spontaneously. She pinches a bit of powder between her forefinger and thumb, then shakes off the excess. She moves her hand to the chosen spot, slides her thumb slowly over the forefinger, which acts like a miniature shovel, and then drops off
25 the powder carefully to make a swirling **arabesque**. The materials may also be sieved through a clenched fist, using fingertips to trace **filigreed** patterns. Lentils, grains, pebbles, and flowers are added for texture and color. The designs glow in sunlight and **coruscate** in reflected moonlight.

Whether an everyday routine or a celebratory ritual, *rangoli* turns a com-
30 mon floor into momentary poetry. Its **fugacious** nature, whereby the designs are swept away with a grass broom at day's end (if they haven't been trampled beforehand), emphasizes the process of creation. Once the beautiful pictures are swept away, only their **specters** linger in the minds of their creators.

Words

adorn
arabesque
coruscate
filigree
fugacious
modest
palpable
prescriptive
sacrosanct
specter

Unlocking Meaning

Each word in this lesson's word list appears in dark type in the selection you just read. Think about how the vocabulary word is used in the selection, then write the letter for the best answer to each question.

1. Which words could best replace *palpable* in line 1?
   (A) easily perceived or obvious   (B) legally recognized
   (C) of no primary significance   (D) free from blemish

   1. _A_

2. Something that is *sacrosanct* (line 2) is _____.
   (A) stale through overuse   (B) unnoticed
   (C) regarded as sacred and inviolable   (D) marked by logical consistency

   2. _C_

3. Which words could best replace *modest* in line 7?
   (A) having similar limitations   (B) free from showiness
   (C) serving to support   (D) providing physical comfort

   3. _____

4. Which word or words could best replace *adorn* in line 11?
   (A) make progress   (B) restrict movement
   (C) decorate   (D) split into parts

   4. _____

5. Something that is *prescriptive* (line 16) is _____.
   (A) suited to one's purpose   (B) characterized by careful evaluation
   (C) caused by suffering   (D) determined by long-standing custom or usage

   5. _____

6. An *arabesque* (line 25) can best be explained as a(n) _____.
   (A) elaborate design   (B) unfavorable condition
   (C) lack of harmony   (D) act of destruction

   6. _____

7. Which word or words can best replace *filigreed* in line 26?
   (A) overbearing   (B) widely used
   (C) unnecessary   (D) intricately ornamented

   7. _____

8. Which word or words can best replace *coruscate* in line 28?
   (A) rust   (B) deteriorate
   (C) sparkle and glitter   (D) evaporate

   8. _____

9. Which word or words can best replace *fugacious* in line 30?
   (A) passing away quickly   (B) revolutionary
   (C) gruesome   (D) uninhibited

   9. _____

10. *Specters* (line 33) can best be described as _____.
    (A) strange or odd aspects   (B) haunting images
    (C) long periods of time   (D) sources of risk

    10. _____

Applying Meaning

Decide which vocabulary word in parentheses best completes the sentence. Then write the sentence, adding the missing word.

1. Tricia regarded her jewelry box as _____; she believed that any attempt by her younger sister to borrow a pair of earrings without asking was an assault. (fugacious; sacrosanct)

   _____

   _____

   _____

2. Seven-year-old Kelly _____ her hair with flowers, then smiled at her reflection in the mirror. (adorned; coruscated)

   _____

   _____

   _____

3. To set off his conservative gray business suits, Mr. Zukroff chose ties with _____ in brilliant blues, purples, and reds. (arabesques; specters)

   _____

   _____

   _____

4. The tension in the room was _____; conversation between the jury members was halting, and their body language was stiff and uncomfortable. (modest; palpable)

   _____

   _____

   _____

5. George Orwell's *1984* is a _____ of a society in which privacy is impossible, truth is replaced with propaganda, and thought and love are punished. (filigree; specter)

   _____

   _____

   _____

Follow the directions below to write a sentence using a vocabulary word.

6. Describe someone who rebels against standardized or traditional techniques in some area of specialization. Use any form of the word *prescriptive.*

_____

_____

_____

7. Comment on a philosophy of life. Use any form of the word *fugacious.*

_____

_____

_____

8. Describe someone who has a moderate or restrained view of his or her accomplishments. Use any form of the word *modest.*

_____

_____

_____

9. Describe a building's ornamentation. Use any form of the word *filigree.*

_____

_____

_____

10. Describe a gemstone that might attract someone's attention. Use any form of the word *coruscate.*

_____

_____

_____

Mastering Meaning

Imagine that you have been hired by a museum to produce a catalog for a new show of antiquities. Choose an ancient object, such as a rug, a weapon, a vase, or a piece of jewelry, and write a catalog entry in which you provide a detailed description as well as a historical narrative. Your goal is to portray this object as vividly as you can. Use some of the words you studied in this lesson.

Name _____

Agreement and disagreement are part of many discussions, regardless of the subject. Although it is ideal when "great minds think alike," the fact that people have different backgrounds, experiences, opinions, and values often places them at cross purposes with one another. The words in this lesson will help you describe both harmonious and antagonistic situations.

Unlocking Meaning

Read the sentences or short passages below. Write the letter for the correct definition of the italicized vocabulary word.

The late president Richard Nixon was an *apologist* for the Vietnam War. He coined the term "the silent majority" to indicate his firm belief that most Americans supported his policies and that those who demonstrated against U.S. involvement in Vietnam amounted to only a noisy minority.

1. (A) soldier
    (B) one who demonstrates loudly and emotionally
    (C) a person who confuses an issue with irrelevant details
    (D) one who defends or justifies something

Because of Archimedes' experiments with buoyancy, we accept as *axiomatic* the observation that when an object placed in water is weighed and its weight in water is compared to its weight out of water, it seems to lose a definite amount in water—an amount equal to the weight of the water it displaces. This principle explains why a boat floats.

2. (A) easily angered
    (B) universally recognized as true
    (C) closely joined
    (D) coinciding in effect

Galileo initially *corroborated* Copernicus's model of the solar system, but he was forced by the Roman Catholic church to renounce his belief. Even though he had witnessed otherwise with his telescope, he was pressured to assert that the Earth stands still, with the Sun revolving around it.

3. (A) supported with other evidence
    (B) seized or captured
    (C) broke down suddenly
    (D) rejected another's findings

Parapsychologists who experiment with extrasensory perception and telekinesis claim that these extraordinary abilities exist. Many scientists *demur*, because such claims cannot be verified with scientific procedures.

4. (A) agree
    (B) pressure by force
    (C) damage the functioning of
    (D) voice opposition

Words

apologist

axiomatic

corroborate

demur

dissuade

extol

fallacy

obsequious

postulate

ruminate

1. _____

2. _____

3. _____

4. _____

Experienced Iditarod runners tried to *dissuade* Gary Paulsen from competing in the grueling Alaska race, but they were not successful. The writer and his team of sled dogs nearly perished during the race.

5. (A) distract in devious ways

    (B) retreat from

    (C) deter someone by persuasion

    (D) pull away with extreme force

5. _____

The newspaper review *extolled* the performance of the Cossack dancers, noting in particular their seemingly impossible leaps and their fancy footwork.

6. (A) criticized

    (B) omitted details about

    (C) praised highly

    (D) provided a basis for

6. _____

Many educators regard as *fallacy* the idea that children should not begin formal education until the age of six. Some claim that youngsters can benefit by taking earlier advantage of their natural language abilities.

7. (A) category of related objects or ideas

    (B) false notion

    (C) fact

    (D) test that uses a single indicator to prompt a decision

7. _____

Ms. Ramapo and her daughters refuse to shop in the new boutique because they resent their browsing being interrupted every few minutes by *obsequious* salespeople.

8. (A) overly attentive

    (B) having a disagreeable disposition

    (C) outstanding

    (D) extremely careful

8. _____

Social scientists in the nineteenth century *postulated* that Western culture was superior to all others and was the standard by which all other cultures should be measured. This erroneous perspective prevented them from gathering objective data.

9. (A) rejected vehemently

    (B) treated carefully

    (C) resisted loudly

    (D) assumed as true

9. _____

Henry Ford wanted everyone to have access to personal transportation. He *ruminated* about ways to accomplish this until he devised the assembly-line technique, by which the Model T automobile and its successors were made available to millions of people.

10. (A) lied

    (B) reflected

    (C) gave a public presentation

    (D) argued

10. _____

Applying Meaning

Write each sentence below. In the space write a form of the word in parentheses. The form of the word in parentheses may be correct.

1. Parents in particular are supporters of Benjamin Franklin's _____ "Early to bed and early to rise, makes a man healthy, wealthy, and wise." (axiomatic)

   _____

   _____

   _____

2. Kings who have divorced their wives for failing to produce a son have held to the _____ that it is the mother who determines the gender of a child. (fallacy)

   _____

   _____

   _____

3. For the purpose of argument, let's accept the _____ that Jupiter might be destroyed by bombarding comets. (postulate)

   _____

   _____

   _____

4. James D. Watson's work with the double helix of DNA was _____ of Francis Crick's experiments in England. (corroborate)

   _____

   _____

   _____

5. Courtiers were expected to show their _____ to the monarch by bowing low over clasped hands and backing out of the throne room. (obsequious)

   _____

   _____

   _____

Each question below contains a vocabulary word from this lesson. Answer each question "yes" or "no" in the space provided.

6. If you always *demur*, are you considered easygoing?

6. _____

7. Would an *apologist* for an organization emphasize its failings?

7. _____

8. Might someone *extol* the talents of a young tenor in his first opera?

8. _____

9. If you were planning a camping trip, might you be *dissuaded* by reports of forest fires in the area you planned to visit?

9. _____

10. If you *ruminate* over a decision, do you decide quickly and easily?

10. _____

For each question you answered "no," write a sentence using the vocabulary word correctly.

_____

_____

_____

_____

_____

_____

_____

_____

_____

Our Living Language

Ruminate, one of the words in this lesson, has a surprising etymology. In Latin, the word *rumen* refers to the first compartment in the stomach of cattle and sheep, in which undigested food is stored until the animals are ready to chew and digest it. Because these ruminant mammals appear to be thoughtful and subdued as they chew their cud, the Latin word *ruminare* began to be used as a metaphor for quiet reflection on a subject. Eventually, the word itself came to mean "ponder" or "muse" when applied to people.

Use the Dictionary: Many other English words have a connection with animals. Look up the definitions and origins of the words below. Then write a brief explanation of the connections between the current meaning of each word and its derivation.

aviation   coward   muscle   pester   porcelain   rostrum

Name _____

The root *-roga-*, from the Latin word *rogare*, means "to ask." When combined with different prefixes and suffixes, this root defines different ways of making requests. The root *-sag-*, from the Latin word *sagire*, means "to perceive." In this lesson you will learn ten words that are related to the ideas of asking and perceiving.

Root	Meaning	English Word
-roga-	to ask	interrogate
-sag-	to perceive	sagacious

Unlocking Meaning

Write the vocabulary word that fits each clue below. Then say the word and write a short definition. Compare your definition and pronunciation with those given on the flash card.

1. This word, from the Latin *surrogare*, can be a noun, adjective, or verb. If you cannot attend a meeting yourself, you might send one of these.

   _____

   _____

   _____

2. This word, which can be either a noun or a verb, begins with the prefix *pre-*, meaning "before." People who can do this are thought to have special powers or a sixth sense.

   _____

   _____

   _____

3. This adjective describes someone who is extremely wise and whom you might ask for advice. It contains the same root as the answer to number 2.

   _____

   _____

   _____

4. This word came to us from the Latin word *abrogare*. You might use this verb when you want to explain why certain rules no longer apply.

   _____

   _____

   _____

Words

- **abrogate**
- **arrogate**
- **derogatory**
- **interrogate**
- **prerogative**
- **presage**
- **prorogue**
- **sagacious**
- **subrogate**
- **surrogate**

5. Your friends will undoubtedly be offended if you make these kinds of remarks about their appearance, sense of humor, or intelligence. They may feel you are "asking" people to think ill of you.

_____

_____

_____

6. This noun has a prefix that means "before." When the governor pardons a convicted criminal, he or she is exercising this.

_____

_____

_____

7. This verb comes from the Latin word *arrogare*. A playground bully or tyrannical ruler might be accused of doing this.

_____

_____

_____

8. This word has the prefix *sub-*, meaning "instead of." You might use this verb when you want to explain how two things are interchangeable.

_____

_____

_____

9. This verb has a prefix that means "between." If you were a police detective, you might do this to a suspect.

_____

_____

_____

10. This verb has a prefix that means "forward." The word might be used to describe how the date of a court hearing was changed.

_____

_____

_____

Applying Meaning

Follow the directions below to write a sentence using a vocabulary word.

1. Explain how a substitute functions in any context other than school. Use any form of the word *surrogate*.

    _____

    _____

    _____

2. Use *sagacious* in a sentence to describe someone whom you respect for his or her perceptive abilities.

    _____

    _____

    _____

3. Comment on a ridiculous law that you would like to see removed from the books. Use any form of the word *abrogate*.

    _____

    _____

    _____

4. Describe a superstition about the weather or the seasons. Use any form of the word *presage*.

    _____

    _____

    _____

5. Comment on the effects of making degrading comments to another person. Use any form of the word *derogatory*.

    _____

    _____

    _____

Read each sentence below. Write "correct" on the answer line if the vocabulary word has been used correctly. Write "incorrect" on the answer line if the vocabulary word has been used incorrectly.

6. The president of the United States has the *prerogative* to veto a bill.

    6. _____

7. The judge *prorogued* the trial to allow the lawyers time to prepare for the case.

    7. _____

8. Mr. Chan changed the beneficiary on his insurance policy, *subrogating* his wife for his parents.

9. *Interrogated* among the knickknacks on her dressing table were several antique perfume bottles.

10. *Arrogation* turned the windswept plains into a virtual garden.

8. _____

9. _____

10. _____

For each word used incorrectly, write a sentence using the word properly.

_____

_____

_____

_____

_____

_____

_____

_____

_____

_____

Our Living Language

The name of a car is an important part of its overall image and marketability. Each year, manufacturers spend millions of dollars researching and developing names that will appeal to customers. Some cars are named after animals, while others take on the identities of romantic places to visit. Many names hint at speed or power; others suggest the status of the rich and famous. The names of smaller, less expensive, and more practical cars imply that purchasers are virtuous and patriotic in buying these vehicles. Think about whether you would be more likely to buy a car called the Desperado or one named the Argosy. Which one appeals more to the image you have of yourself?

Cooperative Learning: With several of your classmates, list as many names of car models as you can, such as Jaguar, El Dorado, Civic, Omni, Millennia, and so forth. Then discuss the connotations of each name and the type of person whose perceptions might be influenced by them.

Name _____

How well do you remember the words you studied in Lessons 1 through 3?
Take the following test covering the words from the last three lessons.

Part 1 Choose the Correct Meaning

Each question below includes a word in capital letters, followed by four words
or phrases. Choose the word or phrase that is <u>closest</u> in meaning to the word
in capital letters. Write the letter for your answer on the line provided.

Sample

S. FINISH	(A) enjoy	(B) complete	**S.** ____**B**____
	(C) destroy	(D) enlarge	

1. PALPABLE   (A) delicious   (B) obvious   1. _____
                 (C) hidden   (D) splendid

2. CORROBORATE   (A) compare   (B) contradict   2. _____
                     (C) confirm   (D) organize

3. ABROGATE   (A) abolish   (B) stimulate   3. _____
              (C) decide   (D) establish

4. RUMINATE   (A) ignore   (B) ransack   4. _____
              (C) meditate   (D) exhilarate

5. DEMUR   (A) hold back   (B) respect   5. _____
          (C) approve   (D) object

6. EXTOL   (A) tax   (B) praise   6. _____
        (C) boast   (D) criticize

7. POSTULATE   (A) assume as true   (B) calculate   7. _____
             (C) generalize   (D) evaluate

8. PROROGUE   (A) confuse   (B) foretell   8. _____
           (C) postpone   (D) recommend

9. SUBROGATE   (A) conquer   (B) obscure   9. _____
            (C) surrender   (D) substitute

10. FUGACIOUS   (A) permanent   (B) fleeting   10. _____
             (C) belligerent   (D) thrifty

Go on to next page. ➤

11. CORUSCATE   (A) wrinkle   (B) orchestrate   11. _____
                      (C) deteriorate   (D) sparkle

12. INTERROGATE   (A) question   (B) insinuate   12. _____
                      (C) respond   (D) bother

13. SAGACIOUS   (A) ignorant   (B) conspicuous   13. _____
                      (C) wise   (D) vicious

14. MODEST   (A) fashionable   (B) inadequate   14. _____
                      (C) ordinary   (D) showy

15. DEROGATORY   (A) descriptive   (B) critical   15. _____
                      (C) complimentary   (D) tolerable

Part 2 *Matching Words and Meanings*

Match the definition in Column B with the word in Column A.
Write the letter of the correct definition on the line provided.

Column A	Column B	
16. sacrosanct	a. predict	16. _____
17. adorn	b. intricate ornamentation	17. _____
18. fallacy	c. haunting image	18. _____
19. presage	d. decorate	19. _____
20. arrogate	e. exclusive right or privilege	20. _____
21. specter	f. sacred and inviolable	21. _____
22. obsequious	g. substitute	22. _____
23. filigree	h. claim or seize	23. _____
24. prerogative	i. fawning	24. _____
25. surrogate	j. mistaken belief	25. _____

Name _____

William Tell: Man or Myth?

William Tell, the national hero of Switzerland, has long been a powerful source of artistic inspiration and the focal point of plays, musical compositions, paintings, and poems. Like Robin Hood, the **intrepid** peasant symbolized the struggle for political and individual freedom. Today, however, hallowed chapters of Swiss history are being rewritten, and Tell has been relegated to the realm of folklore.

According to the **conventional** version of history, the peasants of three cantons (states) in central Switzerland, **incensed** over their brutal repression by the Hapsburg rulers, stormed and destroyed the mighty castles of the Austrians in 1291. Their **impetus** came from William Tell, who refused to make **obeisance** to a governor's hat that was displayed publicly as the symbol of Austrian authority. Viewed as **impertinent**, Tell was **reputedly** punished by having to shoot an arrow through an apple resting on his son's head. Tell is said to have performed the feat but was thrown into chains when he confessed that had he harmed his son, he would have used a second arrow to shoot the governor. Later, while Tell was being taken across Lake Lucerne by the governor and his men to the dungeon in the governor's castle, a violent storm broke out. The governor told Tell to steer the boat, promising him freedom in return for bringing them home safely. Under the **guise** of being helpful, Tell brought the boat to shore, but then quickly jumped out and pushed the boat back into the stormy waters. Realizing that the governor and his men might survive the storm anyway, he stationed himself along the only path to the governor's castle. When the governor appeared, Tell drew his bow and arrow and shot the governor through the heart. Soon after, the peasants gathered in a meadow and took a solemn oath to unite against foreign oppression and to form an **egalitarian** and independent state.

Unfortunately, this uplifting story has almost no foundation in fact. No evidence that William Tell ever existed has been unearthed. Some medievalists believe simply that some of the deeds attributed to him have been culled from other heroic figures or mythical sources. Others conjecture that his origins stemmed from fifteenth-century humanists intent on finding a character who would appeal to the growing Swiss national consciousness. Perhaps William Tell's significance lies in the power that he represents as a **partisan** of the universal passion for freedom.

Words
conventional
egalitarian
guise
impertinent
impetus
incensed
intrepid
obeisance
partisan
reputed

Unlocking Meaning

Each word in this lesson's word list appears in dark type in the selection you just read. Think about how the vocabulary word is used in the selection, then write the letter for the best answer to each question.

1. Which word could best replace *intrepid* in line 3?

   (A) shy   (B) fearless

   (C) dishonest   (D) comical

   1. _____

2. Something that is *conventional* (line 7) can best be explained as _____.

   (A) well-researched   (B) political

   (C) intentionally vague   (D) customary or traditional

   2. _____

3. Which words could best replace *incensed* in line 8?

   (A) extremely angry   (B) inspiring shock

   (C) appearing worn or exhausted (D) thoroughly gratified

   3. _____

4. An *impetus* (line 10) can best be explained as _____.

   (A) something added or gained (B) the condition of being free from control

   (C) a stimulating force   (D) an infectious disease

   4. _____

5. An act of *obeisance* (line 11) can best be explained as a _____.

   (A) negative remark   (B) gesture that expresses respect

   (C) monetary contribution   (D) formal consent

   5. _____

6. Which words could best replace *impertinent* in line 12?

   (A) showing lack of proper respect   (B) full of complications

   (C) insistently repetitive   (D) pleasing in personality

   6. _____

7. Which word could best replace *reputedly* in line 13?

   (A) carefully   (B) formerly

   (C) personally   (D) supposedly

   7. _____

8. A *guise* (line 20) can best be explained as a(n) _____.

   (A) temporary platform   (B) lingering sign of damage

   (C) outward appearance or aspect   (D) large mechanical device

   8. _____

9. Which words could best replace *egalitarian* in line 27?

   (A) marked by vigorous activity (B) characterized by a belief in equal rights for all

   (C) exhibiting an intolerance to others not like oneself   (D) containing material damaging to reputation

   9. _____

10. A *partisan* (line 35) can best be explained as someone who _____.

    (A) fervently supports a cause (B) supervises an activity

    (C) avoids responsibility   (D) prejudges others

    10. _____

Applying Meaning

Decide which word in parentheses best completes the sentence. Then write the sentence, adding the missing word.

1. Used by the Department of War as part of an experiment in 1856, camels were _____ to be effective members of the cavalry. They could carry one-thousand-pound loads, travel thirty or forty miles per day, and go without water for six to ten days. (incensed; reputed)

    _____

    _____

    _____

2. Under the _____ of friendship, Victor Emmanuel II of Italy would present little pieces of himself to favored courtiers. One of his most unusual gifts was a half-inch-long toenail that the royal jeweler had edged with gold and encrusted with diamonds. (advocacy; guise)

    _____

    _____

    _____

3. The Kalapalo Indians, who live on the savannas of central Brazil, have little _____ to change their leisurely lifestyle. They work just several hours a week to provide food, their only need. (impetus; obeisance)

    _____

    _____

    _____

4. _____ by the squat design of the Lyndon Baines Johnson Library, residents of Austin, Texas, tried to block its construction. (Advocated; Incensed)

    _____

    _____

    _____

5. Banary Bhat _____ set out to prove that beekeeping is not dangerous. Placing a queen bee on his cheek, he attracted a swarm of her followers that clung, beardlike, to his face. Bhat could eat dinner, play cards, and do just about anything else without risk. (conventionally; intrepidly)

    _____

    _____

    _____

Read each sentence or short passage below. Write "correct" on the answer line if the vocabulary word has been used correctly. Write "incorrect" on the answer line if the vocabulary word has been used incorrectly.

6. If a woman contracts German measles during the first three months of pregnancy, the disease can cause severe *conventional* defects in the developing fetus.

6. _____

7. In an *egalitarian* government, unlimited control is held by one person.

7. _____

8. *Partisans* of the preservation of shark and whale species provoke the hostility of fishermen who depend on the creatures for their livelihood.

8. _____

9. "Don't be *impertinent*," Roy's grandmother cautioned him. "Take a breath and put your brain in gear before you make an important decision."

9. _____

10. Bowing, a typical way to indicate *obeisance* in many cultures, demonstrates subservience to a superior.

10. _____

For each word used incorrectly, write a sentence using the word properly.

_____

_____

_____

_____

_____

_____

_____

_____

_____

_____

_____

Mastering Meaning

Imagine that the United States Postal Service has relaxed its standards for commemorative stamps so that citizens may now nominate living people for the honor. Write a letter to the postmaster general, making a strong case for someone you believe should be immortalized in this way. Although you may choose a famous person, try to think of someone you admire who might otherwise never achieve fame. Use some of the words you studied in this lesson.

Name _____

First impressions tend to be based on behavior that reflects attitude; most people are attracted to civil, gracious actions while they are repelled by rudeness and ill will. The words in this lesson will help you analyze some of the behaviors that affect you.

Unlocking Meaning

Read the sentences or short passages below. Write the letter for the correct definition of the italicized vocabulary word.

Mr. Jacobson's endless *carping* remarks about the neighborhood boys' long, messy hair alienated many of them.

1. (A) bizarre
   (B) surprisingly impressive
   (C) naggingly critical
   (D) courageous

Before leaving for their new posts, the diplomats were told about the *deferential* treatment they could expect from foreign leaders. Many of these rulers owed a great deal to the United States.

2. (A) courteously respectful
   (B) rude
   (C) marked by informality
   (D) unlucky

It was clear that the seventeen-year-old cat was ill; her normal scampering had been reduced to a *lethargic* sprawl, and she had lost interest in food.

3. (A) serious
   (B) clearly defined
   (C) sluggish
   (D) vigorous

By assuming that immigrants to this country do not speak or understand English, some Americans exhibit an unfair, *patronizing* attitude. They tend to look down on immigrants and think they are uneducated.

4. (A) miserly
   (B) spiteful
   (C) showing great force or power
   (D) characterized by a superior manner

Words

carping

deferential

lethargic

patronizing

phlegmatic

sanctimonious

sanguine

scurrilous

surly

truculent

1. _____

2. _____

3. _____

4. _____

For someone who had a quick temper as a child, Dan has become quite *phlegmatic*. Even his brothers have stopped teasing him because they can't get a reaction from him.

5. (A) easily offended

    (B) having a calm temperament

    (C) worthy of imitation

    (D) obnoxious

5. _____

Joan of Arc was burned at the stake, in part because the English thought her claim that God spoke to her was purely *sanctimonious*.

6. (A) distinct from others

    (B) proper

    (C) pretending religious devotion

    (D) common

6. _____

Beth's *sanguine* nature contradicted her long history of illness. In spite of constant pain, she looked forward to a time when she would be more active.

7. (A) confident; optimistic

    (B) pessimistic

    (C) careful and diligent

    (D) nourishing

7. _____

The restaurant critic for the local newspaper was justifiably fired. While negative reviews are to be expected, his *scurrilous* remarks were uncalled for and embarrassing.

8. (A) flattering

    (B) creative

    (C) pleasing in manner

    (D) abusive and vulgar

8. _____

Incensed by the *surly* behavior of the clerk, Ms. Caine reported him to the manager. She believes that customers deserve courteous treatment, even when returning merchandise.

9. (A) sullenly ill-humored

    (B) profoundly moving

    (C) romantic

    (D) straightforward

9. _____

After being pushed around on the basketball court all afternoon, Stephen was in a *truculent* mood. He felt that if one more person pushed him, he would start swinging. To vent his frustration, he took a long walk.

10. (A) helpless

    (B) disposed to fight

    (C) outwardly extravagant

    (D) refined

10. _____

Applying Meaning

Decide which word in parentheses best completes the sentence. Then write the sentence, adding the missing word.

1. The voters' response to the senator's _____ remarks about his female opponent was to vote him out of office. (lethargic; scurrilous)

   _____

   _____

   _____

2. Greta's _____ remarks caused her classmates to snicker. Even though they knew she went to church every Sunday, they were also aware that she cheated on tests and lied to her parents. (deferential; sanctimonious)

   _____

   _____

   _____

3. Angered by the unfavorable comments of the press, the actor _____ defended her performance. (lethargically; truculently)

   _____

   _____

   _____

4. The champion tennis player has often been criticized for his _____ toward his opponents and the referees. (lethargy; surliness)

   _____

   _____

   _____

5. Even his political opponents honored the elderly former prime minister with their _____ applause. (carping; deferential)

   _____

   _____

   _____

6. By the end of August, Kyle was so bored and _____ that he barely responded to his friends' invitations. (lethargic; patronizing)

   _____

   _____

   _____

Each question below contains a vocabulary word from this lesson. Answer each question "yes" or "no" in the space provided.

7. If you are completely prepared for an upcoming exam, should you have a *sanguine* attitude toward it?

7. _____

8. If you acted *patronizingly* toward a friend, would she consider you supportive?

8. _____

9. Is it difficult to upset a *phlegmatic* person?

9. _____

10. Do people respond favorably to someone who frequently makes *carping* remarks?

10. _____

For each question you answered "no," write a sentence using the vocabulary word correctly.

_____

_____

_____

_____

_____

_____

_____

_____

Cultural Literacy Note

Two words in this lesson have an interesting connection to medieval medicine. During the Middle Ages, physicians believed that the human body was made up of four humors, or fluids: blood (*sanguis* in Latin), phlegm, choler, and black bile. They believed that the relative proportion of these liquids determined not only general health, but disposition as well. For instance, someone with an excess of blood had a ruddy complexion and a hopeful nature and was considered *sanguine*. A *phlegmatic* person was someone with an excess of phlegm who had frequent colds that led to sluggishness.

Cooperative Learning: With a partner, use dictionaries and other references to explore the origins and definitions of the words below. Prepare a brief oral report explaining how these words are related to the medieval theory of humors.

melancholy	choleric	bilious	gall

The Roots -sens- *and* -sent-

Lesson 6 Part A

Name _____

The roots *-sens-* and *-sent-* come from the Latin word *sentire*, meaning "to feel." When combined with different prefixes and suffixes, these roots give us a number of words that concern feeling. The words in this lesson will help you describe and explain physical sensations as well as emotional states.

Root	Meaning	English Word
-sens-	to feel	insensate
-sent-		presentiment

Unlocking Meaning

A vocabulary word appears in italics in each sentence or short passage below. Find the root in the vocabulary word and think about how the word is used in the passage. Then write a definition for the vocabulary word. Compare your definition with the definition on the flash card.

1. Although she remained unconvinced that her students had isolated all the necessary variables, Ms. Boland *assented* to their choice of an experiment for their independent study.

   _____

   _____

   _____

2. To reach a *consensus* in decision-making, the participants must listen to each other carefully, evaluate the alternatives, and make necessary compromises. Only then will everyone be able to accept the results.

   _____

   _____

   _____

3. There is considerable *dissent* in the scientific community over the risk involved in releasing genetically engineered organisms into the environment. Some favor taking the risk, but others oppose it.

   _____

   _____

   _____

4. Juanita's friends accused her of being *insensate*. Even when her dog died, she seemed unaffected.

   _____

   _____

   _____

Words

- **assent**
- **consensus**
- **dissent**
- **insensate**
- **presentiment**
- **resentment**
- **sensibility**
- **sententious**
- **sentimentality**
- **sentinel**

Copyright © Glencoe/McGraw-Hill, a division of The McGraw-Hill Companies, Inc.

5. Clarinda had a *presentiment* that the next day a letter would arrive that would drastically alter her future.

_____

_____

_____

6. Her *resentment* of her younger brother stemmed from her father's favoritism toward him.

_____

_____

_____

7. The television reports on the famine in Africa shocked his *sensibilities*. Reading about it in the newspapers hadn't affected him in the same way.

_____

_____

_____

8. We were all insulted by Carver's *sententious* presentation. We obviously knew the difference between right and wrong by now.

_____

_____

_____

9. Although some people found that the novels of Jane Austen suffered from excessive Victorian *sentimentality*, Ryan thought her books were subtle and understated.

_____

_____

_____

10. During the changing of the guard, the *sentinels* at Buckingham Palace perform precise maneuvers that attract much attention from tourists.

_____

_____

_____

Applying Meaning

Write the vocabulary word that fits each clue below. Then write a sentence using any form of the vocabulary word correctly. You may include the information in the clue.

1. This condition might exist between an employer and employees whose promised bonuses did not materialize.

   _____

   _____

   _____

2. Because of differing opinions, values, and experiences, this is often difficult for groups to achieve.

   _____

   _____

   _____

3. In a large office building, this person may be employed to sit in the lobby after hours.

   _____

   _____

   _____

4. Some people think that love songs and ballads suffer from this.

   _____

   _____

   _____

5. This is affected when a patient is given an anesthetic.

   _____

   _____

   _____

Rewrite each sentence below. Replace the underlined word or words with a vocabulary word or a form of the vocabulary word.

6. Even though people give human characteristics to their cars by naming them, most know that cars are <u>not capable of feeling.</u>

_____

_____

7. Victor seethed with <u>anger and bitterness</u> when his teammates accused him of faking an injury.

_____

_____

8. A person who repeatedly has <u>feelings that something is about to happen</u> may be described as having a sixth sense.

_____

_____

9. The interior designer needed her client's <u>agreement</u> before placing the order for the furniture.

_____

_____

10. Mali's <u>self-righteous and moralizing</u> speech bored us to death.

_____

_____

Bonus Word

cynical

Cynicism was the name for the theories of the Greek philosopher Antisthenes. *Cynical,* meaning "doubting the goodness or sincerity of others," comes from his disciples' rude manners and their scorn for the motives, virtue, or integrity of other people.

Write a Character Sketch: Choose one of the words below and re-search its origin. Then write a brief description of a person who exhibits the emotional state of the word you have researched.

feisty   giddy   hysterical   jovial

Name _____

How well do you remember the words you studied in Lessons 4 through 6?
Take the following test covering the words from the last three lessons.

Part 1 Antonyms

Each question below includes a word in capital letters, followed by four
words or phrases. Choose the word or phrase that is most nearly <u>opposite</u>
in meaning to the word in capital letters. Consider all choices before deciding on your answer. Write the letter for your answer on the line provided.

Sample

S. HIGH	(A) cold	(B) simple	**S.** ___C___
	(C) low	(D) foolish	

1. INTREPID   (A) courageous   (B) weary   1. _____
                   (C) cowardly   (D) sophisticated

2. LETHARGIC   (A) energetic   (B) sluggish   2. _____
                   (C) dependable   (D) greedy

3. DISSENT   (A) respect   (B) agreement   3. _____
                   (C) disagreement   (D) accumulation

4. SURLY   (A) sly   (B) confident   4. _____
                   (C) amiable   (D) sullen

5. CONSENSUS   (A) agreement   (B) faithfulness   5. _____
                   (C) discouragement   (D) disagreement

6. INCENSED   (A) pleased   (B) very angry   6. _____
                   (C) thoughtful   (D) predictable

7. OBEISANCE   (A) bow   (B) slenderness   7. _____
                   (C) reverence   (D) disrespect

8. PARTISAN   (A) hindrance   (B) opponent   8. _____
                   (C) instructor   (D) supporter

9. DEFERENTIAL   (A) obedient   (B) disrespectful   9. _____
                   (C) considerate   (D) flawless

10. SANGUINE   (A) optimistic   (B) unreasonable   10. _____
                   (C) merciful   (D) pessimistic

Go on to next page. ➤

11. ASSENT   (A) discredit   (B) concur

                  (C) disagree   (D) proclaim   11. _____

12. TRUCULENT   (A) amiable   (B) corrupt

                    (C) belligerent   (D) dependable   12. _____

13. SCURRILOUS   (A) abusive   (B) polite

                    (C) conscientious   (D) distasteful   13. _____

14. IMPERTINENT   (A) dictatorial   (B) insolent

                    (C) excitable   (D) respectful   14. _____

15. SANCTIMONIOUS   (A) complimentary   (B) logical

                    (C) sincere   (D) self-righteous   15. _____

Part 2 Matching Words and Meanings

Match the definition in Column B with the word in Column A.
Write the letter of the correct definition on the line provided.

Column A	Column B	
16. conventional	a. guard	16. _____
17. carping	b. driving force	17. _____
18. resentment	c. unemotional	18. _____
19. sentinel	d. unreasonably critical	19. _____
20. guise	e. bitterness	20. _____
21. phlegmatic	f. having a superior manner	21. _____
22. sententious	g. outward appearance	22. _____
23. impetus	h. moralizing	23. _____
24. patronizing	i. ability to believe or feel	24. _____
25. sensibility	j. customary	25. _____

Name _____

Meaningful Measurement

At some point in human history, people shifted from being hunters and gatherers of the food and materials they required to a more permanent society of farmers and traders. The degree of change encompassed by this shift was staggering. For one thing, it was no longer necessary for each
5   individual or family to secure all that was necessary for survival. If one person was good at catching fish but a failure at growing corn, the extra fish could be traded for some of a neighbor's extra corn. It wasn't long before this practice **engendered** questions and arguments about how many fish were worth how much corn.

10   In societies of every kind, such **controversy** has almost always been decided by the strongest or most powerful person. So it is not surprising that many units of measure were based on the leader's body. One of the earliest examples of this, the cubit (the distance from the tip of the middle finger to the point of the elbow of an Egyptian pharaoh), was used in
15   the construction of the pyramids. However, as pharaohs came and went, the system of measurement was thrown **askew**. Not all pharaohs were the same size; some were even small boys. A more familiar unit of measure, the foot, was based on the length of a British king's foot. This **chaotic** approach also brought us units of measurement such as the rod, the
20   chain, the karat, and the gill. Since each unit of measurement was arrived at independently, the number of feet in, for example, a rod or a yard was determined by pure chance.

In the last decade of the eighteenth century, the French Revolution resulted in the **dissolution** of the monarchy. Some scientists realized that,
25   because everything else was changing, they had a unique opportunity to impose order on the **archaic** system of measurement, which they **deplored**, and to establish a more appropriate and more **coherent** system for modern science and society. They knew that the **crux** of their problem was the variance in units of measure, so they decided to **predicate** the
30   new units of measure on nature. For the basis of their system, they chose a tiny fraction of the distance from the equator to the North Pole. They named this unit the meter. For ease of computation, they divided the meter into ten subdivisions called decimeters. Decimeters were divided into centimeters, and centimeters into millimeters. Thus was born what
35   we now call the metric system, which is used by people all over the world.

Words

archaic

askew

chaotic

coherent

controversy

crux

deplore

dissolution

engender

predicate

Each word in this lesson's word list appears in dark type in the selection
you just read. Think about how the vocabulary word is used in the selection, then write the letter for the best answer to each question.

1. In line 8 the word *engendered* means _____.   1. _____
   (A) eliminated   (B) replaced
   (C) ridiculed   (D) produced

2. Which word could best replace *controversy* in line 10?   2. _____
   (A) harmony   (B) conversation
   (C) debate   (D) enjoyment

3. In line 16, the word *askew* means _____.   3. _____
   (A) straight   (B) out of line
   (C) into the legal system   (D) in an orderly arrangement

4. A *chaotic* approach (line 18) is _____.   4. _____
   (A) full of confusion   (B) fascinating
   (C) clever   (D) logical

5. Which word or words could best replace *dissolution* in line 24?   5. _____
   (A) disintegration   (B) elevation to greater importance
   (C) postponement   (D) religious worship

6. Which word or words could best replace *archaic* in line 26?   6. _____
   (A) mathematical   (B) old and outdated
   (C) modern   (D) French

7. In line 27, *deplored* means _____.   7. _____
   (A) honored   (B) despised
   (C) feared   (D) secretly promoted

8. Which word or words could best replace *coherent* in line 27?   8. _____
   (A) logically organized   (B) strange
   (C) expensive   (D) complicated

9. Which word or words could best replace *crux* in line 28?   9. _____
   (A) confusing formula   (B) advertisement
   (C) argument   (D) central point

10. In line 29, the word *predicate* means _____.   10. _____
    (A) disguise   (B) force
    (C) place   (D) base

Applying Meaning

Follow the directions below to write a sentence using a vocabulary word.

1. Describe a city or state law. Use the word *archaic* in your description.

_____

_____

_____

2. Think of a club or organization that no longer exists. Describe it, using any form of the word *dissolution.*

_____

_____

_____

3. Write a sentence about a fad in clothing or a popular entertainer. Use any form of the word *controversy.*

_____

_____

_____

4. Tell about an attitude or idea with which you disagree. Use any form of the word *deplore.*

_____

_____

_____

5. Describe a scene one might observe in a classroom after the teacher leaves the room. Use the word *chaotic.*

_____

_____

_____

6. Describe a school rule or scientific law. Use any form of the word *predicate.*

_____

_____

_____

Read each sentence below. Write "correct" on the answer line if the vocabulary word has been used correctly. Write "incorrect" on the answer line if the vocabulary word has been used incorrectly.

7. I couldn't understand Mr. Washington's explanation because his reasons were so *coherent*.

7. _____

8. The *crux* of the club's problems lies in the lack of money in the treasury.

8. _____

9. The adventurer lost her way while *deploring* the Amazon jungle.

9. _____

10. Without the support of the United States, the *dissolution* of the agreement seemed certain.

10. _____

11. Jonathan liked wearing his baseball cap slightly *askew*.

11. _____

12. At a recent city council meeting, the issue of prohibiting overnight parking was placed on the *engender*.

12. _____

For each word used incorrectly, write a sentence using the word properly.

_____

_____

_____

_____

_____

_____

_____

_____

_____

_____

Mastering Meaning

Think about a unit of measurement you might want to add to our system. For example, you might think of a unit for measuring how confident you feel about a test. You might call such a unit a *brainert,* with 1.0 on the brainert scale being very low confidence and 10.0 being very high confidence. How would you measure the number of brainerts you have for a given exam? Explain your system in a short composition. Use some of the words you studied in this lesson.

Lesson
8
Part A

Name _____

Criticism has both positive and negative connotations. When used as a way of evaluating strengths and weaknesses, constructive criticism can play an important role in changing behavior, attitudes, and skills. When used to condemn, blame, or make fun of someone, however, unfavorable criticism may produce defensiveness and hard feelings. This lesson will familiarize you with the vocabulary of criticism.

Unlocking Meaning

Read the sentences or short passages below. Write the letter for the correct definition of the italicized vocabulary word.

The physical torture that is practiced against political prisoners in other countries is *anathema* to me.

1. (A) an ideal that serves as a pattern
    (B) normal outgrowth
    (C) appreciation
    (D) something that is intensely disliked

When Bobby ate several grapes from the supermarket display, his mother *chastised* him, explaining that snacking without paying was the same as shoplifting.

2. (A) talked freely
    (B) criticized or punished
    (C) prevented
    (D) commanded

Originally, the paintings of the French impressionists were *deprecated* by the critics and the public. More familiar with hard-edged realism, they laughed at the indistinct outlines and pastel colors.

3. (A) disapproved of
    (B) reduced in scale
    (C) given a rave review
    (D) improved

Nazi tactics directed against Jews and other "enemies" of the Third Reich should have provoked *disapprobation* from the rest of the world. Instead, many countries remained silent.

4. (A) apathy
    (B) disinterest
    (C) interest
    (D) disapproval

Words

anathema

chastise

deprecate

disapprobation

invective

recriminate

reproach

reproof

trenchant

vituperative

1. _____

2. _____

3. _____

4. _____

The longer the argument went on, the more appalling it became.
Although the two businessmen had begun with logical points to make, they
were soon reduced to hurling *invective* at one another.

5. (A) philosophy
   (B) diligent research
   (C) abusive language
   (D) compliments

5. _____

When Elsa blamed Gretchen for breaking the vase, Gretchen
recriminated.

6. (A) paid a visit to
   (B) accused in return
   (C) passed imperceptibly by
   (D) articulated feelings to

6. _____

Devora's parents were not angry about her poor math grade; however, they
did *reproach* her for her inadequate preparation.

7. (A) criticize
   (B) spoil
   (C) assess
   (D) indulge

7. _____

During the presidential campaign of 1884, Grover Cleveland expected
reproof for having hired a substitute to fight in the Civil War.

8. (A) a joining of causes
   (B) physical or mental exertion
   (C) a blow from a whip
   (D) disapproval

8. _____

Ogden Nash is well known for his sophisticated wit and *trenchant* satire.

9. (A) generous
   (B) favorable
   (C) cutting
   (D) legally obligated

9. _____

"You would think that he had been the model for the portrait," said John.
"Otherwise, there seems to be no explanation for his *vituperative* assault on
the artist and her work."

10. (A) verbally abusive
    (B) rambling
    (C) pertinent and fitting
    (D) habitual

10. _____

Applying Meaning

Write each sentence below. In the space write a form of the word in parentheses. The form of the word in parentheses may be correct.

1. Barry's _____ editorial about his classmates not taking part in volunteer activities in the community had a strong positive influence on many students. (deprecate)

   _____

   _____

   _____

2. Carmelita's reputation as a babysitter is beyond _____. (reproach)

   _____

   _____

   _____

3. His _____ at the hearing was directed against rock musicians, whom he accused of polluting the minds of children. (trenchant)

   _____

   _____

   _____

4. The _____ exchanged by the cousins surprised even their mothers. (vituperative)

   _____

   _____

   _____

5. Because _____ tends to arouse purely emotional responses in readers, try to keep your persuasive writing well reasoned and objective. (invective)

   _____

   _____

   _____

Each question below contains a vocabulary word from this lesson. Answer each question "yes" or "no" in the space provided.

6. Does a physician give the patient *anathema* before an operation?　　6. _____

7. Would you be happy to get a *reproof* from your geometry teacher?　　7. _____

8. Is being "grounded" for returning home after curfew considered *chastisement?*　　8. _____

9. Does the U.S. Congress have a committee to approve *disapprobations* of public funds?　　9. _____

10. Would *recriminations* tend to perpetuate an argument?　　10. _____

For each word used incorrectly, write a sentence using the word properly.

_____

_____

_____

_____

_____

_____

_____

_____

_____

Bonus Word

sarcasm

Sarcasm, which means "a cutting, often ironic remark intended to wound," comes from the Greek word *sarkazein,* meaning "to bite the lips in rage." Since sarcasm's goal often is to make its victim the object of contempt or ridicule, it tends not to be as effective as constructive criticism.

Cooperative Learning: With a partner, think of a situation in which criticism of some sort leads to a conflict. Plan two role-plays that illustrate the outcome: the first should involve sarcasm and invective, while the second should indicate a more well-reasoned approach. Perform your role-plays for the class and discuss which would be more effective in resolving the conflict.

Name _____

The root *-gno-*, from the Greek word *gignoskein*, means "to know." The root *-sci-*, from the Latin word *scire*, also means "to know." When combined with different prefixes and suffixes, these roots give us a number of words that share the idea of possessing understanding. In this lesson you will learn ten words whose meanings have something to do with knowledge and awareness.

Root	Meaning	English Word
-gno-	to know	prognosis
-sci-	to know	omniscient

Unlocking Meaning

Words
cognizant
conscientious
omniscient
physiognomy
plebiscite
precognition
prescient
prognosis
prognosticate
unconscionable

Write the vocabulary word that fits each clue below. Then say the word and write a short definition. Compare your definition and pronunciation with those given on the flash card.

1. This adjective has a prefix that means "not" and could be used to describe child abuse or the behavior of a hit-and-run driver.

   _____

   _____

   _____

2. This noun begins with the prefix *physio-*, meaning "nature." If you want to be an expert in judging this, you will need to be a careful observer of people's faces.

   _____

   _____

   _____

3. This noun has a root that comes from the Latin word *plebs*, meaning "the people." This word applies to the way people in a state decide important issues.

   _____

   _____

   _____

4. This noun has a prefix that means "before." If you possess this, you may be able to avoid dangerous situations.

   _____

   _____

   _____

5. This adjective begins with the prefix *omni-*, meaning "all." It is sometimes used to describe God.

_____

_____

_____

6. This noun has a variation on the *pre-* prefix. Doctors explain this to help sick patients understand what might lie ahead.

_____

_____

_____

7. This adjective also has a prefix meaning "before." Fortunetellers really deserve to be called this.

_____

_____

_____

8. This adjective describes someone who is guided by his or her conscience. Most employers prefer to hire this type of person.

_____

_____

_____

9. This word is always a verb. If you watch a weather reporter do this on television, you can learn what the weather will be like tomorrow.

_____

_____

_____

10. This word is always an adjective. If you are this, you know what is going on.

_____

_____

_____

Applying Meaning

Read each sentence or short passage below. Write "correct" on the answer line if the vocabulary word has been used correctly. Write "incorrect" on the answer line if the vocabulary word has been used incorrectly.

1. Faith Popcorn has an unparalleled ability to *prognosticate* what Americans will be doing in the next ten years. The marketing expert predicted both the fitness and the "couch potato" trends.

2. Two days before the exam, Jeremy had the *precognition* that everyone but him would pass.

3. The lake contained an abundance of *plebiscites*. Swimmers often had to pick them off their legs and arms.

4. The mayor's *prognosis* for the city's financial future is bleak.

5. Because he was not present at the nominating-committee meeting, Corey was *cognizant* that the committee nominated him for president.

6. The city council members bankrupted Tatesville with their *unconscionable* spending on expensive "fact-finding" trips.

7. A person described as *omniscient* is considered to be all-knowing.

8. *Prescient* individuals make natural scholars because of their in-depth understanding of history.

9. A *conscientious* teacher tries to return papers within a week.

10. School rules require every player to have a *physiognomy* at the start of the season.

1. _____

2. _____

3. _____

4. _____

5. _____

6. _____

7. _____

8. _____

9. _____

10. _____

For each word used incorrectly, write a sentence using the word properly.

_____

_____

_____

_____

_____

_____

_____

_____

_____

_____

_____

_____

The Test of Standard Written English is used by colleges to place students in the appropriate English courses. The test covers grammar, usage, mechanics, and style.

One type of question on this test is sentence correction. Given a sentence and alternative versions of the underlined part of it, you are to select the correct version. Choice A is always the same as the original and means "make no change."

Sample

> **S.** Amazingly, modern physics and chemistry <u>has been helped by alchemists' accidental discoveries.</u>
>
> **S.** _____ **B** _____
>
> (A) has been helped by alchemists' accidental discoveries.
> (B) have been helped by alchemists' accidental discoveries.
> (C) were helped by alchemist's accidental discoveries.
> (D) had been helped by alchemist's accidental discovery.
> (E) has been helped by alchemist's accidental discovery.

The best way to approach this kind of test item is to read the sample sentence and determine whether it is correct or incorrect. If you decide it is incorrect, think about how you would change it. Then look for the answer that matches yours.

Practice: Write the letter of the correct answer for the following test items.

1. Minstrels and troubadours <u>once sang popular songs for the citizens of cities and villages traveling around the country.</u>

   1. _____

   (A) once sang popular songs for the citizens of cities and villages traveling around the country.
   (B) once have sung popular songs for the citizens of cities and villages traveling around the country.
   (C) used to sing popular songs for the citizens of cities and villages traveling around the country.
   (D) once sang popular songs traveling around the country for the citizens of cities and villages.
   (E) traveling around the country once sang popular songs for the citizens of cities and villages.

2. Geoffrey Chaucer probably knew <u>that he was less likely to bore his readers with a wide variety of characters than with only a few.</u>

   2. _____

   (A) that he was less likely to bore his readers with a wide variety of characters than with only a few.
   (B) that he was least likely to bore his readers with a wide variety of characters than with only a few.
   (C) than he was lesser likely to bore his readers with a wide variety of characters than with only a few.
   (D) that he was less likely to bore his readers only with a wide variety of characters than a few.
   (E) that he was less likely to bore his readers with a wide variety of characters rather than only with a few.

Name _____

How well do you remember the words you studied in Lessons 7 through 9? Take the following test covering the words from the last three lessons.

Part 1 Choose the Correct Meaning

Each question below includes a word in capital letters, followed by four words or phrases. Choose the word or phrase that is <u>closest</u> in meaning to the word in capital letters. Write the letter for your answer on the line provided.

Sample

S. FINISH	(A) enjoy	(B) complete	S. ___**B**___
	(C) destroy	(D) enlarge	

1. TRENCHANT   (A) hazardous   (B) cutting   1. _____
                   (C) vague   (D) momentary

2. OMNISCIENT   (A) ignorant   (B) perilous   2. _____
                   (C) all-knowing   (D) all-powerful

3. UNCONSCIONABLE   (A) comatose   (B) irrepressible   3. _____
                   (C) unscrupulous   (D) obstinate

4. ARCHAIC   (A) very old   (B) exquisite   4. _____
                   (C) modern   (D) strenuous

5. COHERENT   (A) logically ordered   (B) disorganized   5. _____
                   (C) cooperative   (D) observant

6. DEPRECATE   (A) praise   (B) belittle   6. _____
                   (C) appreciate   (D) destroy

7. REPROACH   (A) subdue   (B) rest   7. _____
                   (C) push away   (D) scold

8. CONSCIENTIOUS   (A) alert   (B) reliable   8. _____
                   (C) dishonest   (D) noticeable

9. COGNIZANT   (A) logical   (B) uninformed   9. _____
                   (C) aware   (D) capable

10. ASKEW   (A) straight   (B) industrious   10. _____
                   (C) perceptive   (D) awry

Go on to next page. ➤

11. CHAOTIC   (A) confused   (B) orderly   11. _____
(C) tragic   (D) harmful

12. ANATHEMA   (A) emotional disorder   (B) bodily structure   12. _____
(C) blessing   (D) something or someone disliked

13. DISAPPROBATION   (A) disagreement   (B) disapproval   13. _____
(C) catastrophe   (D) handicap

14. DEPLORE   (A) banish   (B) regret   14. _____
(C) overthrow   (D) contradict

15. CHASTISE   (A) compliment   (B) pursue   15. _____
(C) punish   (D) abandon

Part 2 Matching Words and Meanings

Match the definition in Column B with the word in Column A.
Write the letter of the correct definition on the line provided.

Column A	Column B	
16. controversy	a. facial features	16. _____
17. invective	b. able to foresee events	17. _____
18. physiognomy	c. dispute	18. _____
19. prognosis	d. sharp disapproval	19. _____
20. crux	e. answer an accusation by accusing	20. _____
21. reproof	f. abusive language	21. _____
22. plebiscite	g. to cause to exist	22. _____
23. prescient	h. most important point	23. _____
24. recriminate	i. direct vote by the people	24. _____
25. engender	j. prediction of the outcome of a disease	25. _____

Name _____

Stick Style

Between the end of the Civil War and the beginning of the Great Depression, industrialists, financiers, and railroad builders flocked to northern New York State to build family vacation retreats in the **redolent** forests of the Adirondack Mountains. Situated on enormous tracts of land
5   that often exceeded several hundred acres, these luxurious retreats— called Great Camps by their owners—often included not only the main residence but other buildings such as greenhouses and ice houses. The Great Camps fit the wealthy socialites' **romantic** notion of retreating to the simple life in the unspoiled wilderness.

10   **Rustic** designs compatible with the environment emerged as a distinctive regional building style. As in other forested regions of the world, logs were readily available and served as the primary construction material. Stone carried from nearby quarries was used for chimneys and foundations, and wrought iron from local forges provided hardware. Only glass and furni-
15   ture had to be hauled by stagecoach or wagon.

Over time, the builders learned to take the necessary precautions to pro-tect against the capricious weather of the region—rains lasting for weeks or blizzards materializing out of sunny autumn skies. Logs for the walls were **fastidiously** chosen for straightness, shape, and taper. After being flat-
20   tened and joined tightly, they were chinked with a caulking of hemp or plaster to keep out the wind-driven rain and snow. Oversized timbers sup-ported roofs that had to bear multiple feet of drifted snow. Extending far beyond the exterior walls, the roofs **precluded** ice and snow from building up against the foundation walls. While still serving a **functional** purpose,
25   these extended gables also allowed for verandas that wrapped around the structures, providing a setting for social activities.

The interiors of the buildings were showplaces for luxurious **accoutrements**, conveying an atmosphere of **prepossessing** wealth while maintaining the necessary degree of rusticity. Round, polished ceiling beams, tongue-and-
30   groove pine planks, and stone fireplaces were the rough background for elegant furnishings.

The Great Camps of the Adirondacks represent a unique episode in American architectural history. During a relatively short period, the builders succeeded in creating a style that was widely copied; however, the
35   copies rarely achieved the elaboration or refinement of the Adirondack **prototypes**. While only a few of these homes exist today, their **patina** of age offers a tangible and appealing reminder of a vanished lifestyle and the attempt to live harmoniously with nature.

Words
accoutrements
fastidious
functional
patina
preclude
prepossessing
prototype
redolent
romantic
rustic

Unlocking Meaning

Each word in this lesson's word list appears in dark type in the selection you just read. Think about how the vocabulary word is used in the selection, then write the letter for the best answer to each question.

1. Something that is *redolent* (line 3) can best be described as _____.
   (A) lazy or sluggish   (B) fragrant
   (C) faded   (D) capable of being molded

   1. _____

2. Which word or words could best replace *romantic* in line 8?
   (A) tough   (B) free from illness
   (C) elaborate   (D) idealized

   2. _____

3. Which word or words could best replace *rustic* in line 10?
   (A) typical of country life   (B) destructive
   (C) unworkable   (D) typical of city life

   3. _____

4. Which word could best replace *fastidiously* in line 19?
   (A) unquestioningly   (B) inaudibly
   (C) exactingly   (D) quickly

   4. _____

5. Something that is *precluded* (line 23) is _____.
   (A) created   (B) prevented
   (C) easily disturbed   (D) captured

   5. _____

6. Something that is *functional* (line 24) can best be explained as _____.
   (A) designed for a particular use   (B) having a poor reputation
   (C) showing leniency   (D) newly acquired

   6. _____

7. *Accoutrements* (line 27) can best be explained as _____.
   (A) inappropriate language   (B) restraining or blocking actions
   (C) negative comments   (D) items of equipment or furnishings

   7. _____

8. Which words could best replace *prepossessing* in line 28?
   (A) unduly curious   (B) lacking flavor
   (C) serving to impress   (D) newly acquired

   8. _____

9. A *prototype* (line 36) can best be explained as _____.
   (A) an original form serving as a basis for others   (B) stimulation of the mind to a high level of activity
   (C) an inadequate supply   (D) a course of action that one intends to follow

   9. _____

10. Which words could best replace *patina* in line 36?
    (A) punishment that is imposed by another   (B) power affecting a course of events
    (C) change in appearance produced by long use   (D) lack of loyalty

    10. _____

Applying Meaning

Decide which word in parentheses best completes the sentence.
Then write the sentence, adding the missing word.

1. The flowerpots that decorate the patio each summer have acquired a
_____ of moss. (patina; prototype)

_____

_____

_____

2. Wealthy Ms. Carmichael possessed all of the _____ of her social position: the huge house, the fancy car, and the rooms full of clothing and
jewelry. (accoutrements; patinas)

_____

_____

_____

3. _____ memories of bygone holidays linger in Grandmother's kitchen.
(Fastidious; Redolent)

_____

_____

_____

4. The new store offers a _____ assortment of twig furniture, gardening
tools, plaid blankets, and papier-mâché vegetables.
(preclusive; rustic)

_____

_____

_____

5. Maurice was so _____ dressed that even the bows of his shoelaces were
perfectly symmetrical. (fastidiously; functionally)

_____

_____

_____

6. Although Ariel was talented in producing decorative objects, she concentrated her efforts on creating _____ objects and plates that could be used daily. (functional; prepossessing)

_____

_____

_____

7. Before applying for a patent, an inventor must create a _____ of the intended product. (patina; prototype)

_____

_____

_____

8. Miranda's _____ manner made her popular with both students and teachers. (prepossessing; romantic)

_____

_____

_____

9. Many people have _____ notions about the Old West; they acknowledge the adventure rather than the hard life that the pioneers led. (romantic; fastidious)

_____

_____

_____

10. Taking an art workshop is not a _____ to enrolling in a mechanical-drawing class. (preclusion; redolence)

_____

_____

_____

Mastering Meaning

Imagine that you are in charge of arranging a class trip to the country. Where will you go? Why have you chosen this location? Make your recommendation in a short report. Use some of the words you studied in this lesson.

Lesson
11
Part A

Name _____

Have you ever been full of energy one day and too exhausted to move the next? Would you characterize yourself as a couch potato or a fitness nut? Are you more apt to walk a block or wait for a ride? Your level of activity or inactivity probably varies with your mood, the weather, the circumstances, and other factors. The words in this lesson will help you characterize both vigorous and less active pursuits.

Unlocking Meaning

Words
alacrity
celerity
ennui
indolent
languor
lissome
quiescent
sedulous
somnolence
soporific

Read the sentences or short passages below. Write the letter for the correct definition of the italicized vocabulary word.

Dwayne's *alacrity* today was unusual and surprising. Usually, he argues or pouts when we have to visit our relatives.

　　1. (A) freshness
　　　　(B) clever plan
　　　　(C) eagerness
　　　　(D) tolerant viewpoint

Tanita accepted the task with *celerity*. Before the request was completed, she was clearing the table.

　　2. (A) foolish talk
　　　　(B) an overbearing manner
　　　　(C) swiftness of action
　　　　(D) a negative attitude

Automobile associations offer suggestions about how drivers can avoid the *ennui* that often accompanies long car trips. They recommend listening to the radio or tapes and making brief stops for rest and refreshment.

　　3. (A) inflexibility
　　　　(B) disgust
　　　　(C) unpredictability
　　　　(D) boredom

Cheryl was often accused of being *indolent* because she spent most of her summers lying in a hammock either reading or dozing.

　　4. (A) energetic
　　　　(B) reluctant to exert oneself
　　　　(C) incompetent
　　　　(D) unconscious

1. _____

2. _____

3. _____

4. _____

Bruce's *languor* was contagious. Even his visiting cousins claimed they were too tired to climb to the top of the monument.

5. (A) interpretation
   (B) politeness
   (C) specific range of skills
   (D) sluggishness

5. _____

Both dancers and gymnasts must be especially *lissome*. They often spend an hour warming up before a meet or performance so that they do not strain their muscles and tendons.

6. (A) properly qualified
   (B) lonesome
   (C) limber; able to move with ease
   (D) confident

6. _____

In the heat of the day, the inhabitants of the small fishing village were *quiescent*. Even the dogs seemed to be taking a nap.

7. (A) quiet and still
   (B) temperate
   (C) customary
   (D) believable and tangible

7. _____

On New Year's Eve, the *sedulous* student resolved to be at the top of her class by the end of the semester. She planned to study three hours every night and to spend Saturdays at the library.

8. (A) diligent; hardworking
   (B) definite
   (C) generous
   (D) insistently demanding

8. _____

Somnolence can be one of the side effects of taking antibiotics. It's best not to drive or operate machinery if the medication affects you that way.

9. (A) warmth
   (B) drowsiness
   (C) hyperactivity
   (D) rescue from danger

9. _____

For some people, New Age music is *soporific*. The quiet melodies help them relax.

10. (A) alarming
    (B) inducing sleep
    (C) boring
    (D) overwhelming

10. _____

Applying Meaning

Follow the directions below to write a sentence using a vocabulary word.

1. Explain how someone you know accomplished a difficult task. Use any form of the word *sedulous*.

_____

_____

_____

2. Describe how a person's laziness can affect others. Use any form of the word *indolent*.

_____

_____

_____

3. Describe a technique you use when you cannot fall asleep. Use any form of the word *soporific*.

_____

_____

_____

4. Comment on a person's willingness to take on a challenging task. Use any form of the word *alacrity*.

_____

_____

_____

5. Comment on a gymnast's performance. Use any form of the word *lissome*.

_____

_____

_____

6. Describe the effect when a disturbingly loud noise has ended. Use any form of the word *quiescent*.

_____

_____

_____

7. Describe the effect of summer heat on an animal. Use any form of the word *languor.*

_____

_____

_____

8. Comment on the speed and efficiency of someone capable of accomplishing a great deal. Use the word *celerity.*

_____

_____

_____

9. Explain the effect that a lack of organized activity has on a child. Use the word *ennui.*

_____

_____

_____

10. Describe some aspect of nature during the heat of the late afternoon. Use any form of the word *somnolence.*

_____

_____

_____

Cultural Literacy Note

Somnolence, which means "drowsiness," is derived from the Latin word *somnus,* which means "sleep." Somnus, the god of sleep in Roman mythology, was the son of Nox (night), the brother of Mors (death), and the father of Morpheus, the god of sleep and dreams.

Prepare an Oral Report: The names of many of the planets in our solar system also come from classical mythology. Use a dictionary of mythology or of word origins to do research about each planet's name and to prepare an oral report.

Name _____

The root *-fac-* comes from the Latin word *facere,* meaning "to make" or "to do." This root also appears in English words as *-fec-, -fic-, -feas-,* and *-feit-.* When combined with other word parts, this root gives us a number of words that share the idea of creating, performing, and producing.

Root	Meaning	English Word
-fac-	to make, to do	facile

Unlocking Meaning

A vocabulary word appears in italics in each short passage below. Find the root in the vocabulary word and think about how the word is used in the passage. Then write a definition for the vocabulary word. Compare your definition with the definition on the flash card.

1. Gerald's British accent was only an *affectation* he developed after visiting London for three days. In spite of his friends' teasing, he wanted to retain his adopted idioms and pronunciations to try to impress people.

   _____

   _____

   _____

2. Althea demonstrated the *efficacy* of her plan to sell the new videos by citing the enormous response to her direct-mail catalog. Whereas a typical response is less than 10 percent, 42 percent of the recipients called the 800 number for more information.

   _____

   _____

   _____

3. Chin has a *facile* mind when it comes to mathematics. No matter what problem the teacher assigns, he quickly and easily completes it.

   _____

   _____

   _____

4. Many consumers buy spray cans of *factitious* pine fragrance to deodorize their homes. While the smell is pleasant, it cannot match the real pine fragrance found in the forest.

   _____

   _____

Words

- affectation
- efficacy
- facile
- factitious
- feasible
- officious
- proficient
- prolific
- suffice
- surfeit

5. Jennifer had studied the opponents' game plan and developed what her coach thought was a *feasible* strategy for defeating them. But they would have to wait until the game started to see if it really worked.

_____

_____

_____

6. *Officious* friends and relatives almost caused Mariel to cancel her trip to Brazil. The more they warned her about the dangers she might encounter, the more she wished they would mind their own business.

_____

_____

_____

7. The critics praised the *proficient* pianist's renderings of the challenging concerto. They claimed her fingers slid over the keys like butter melted over a warm croissant.

_____

_____

_____

8. Both Stephen King and Dean Koontz are extraordinarily *prolific* writers who publish at least one book per year. Most writers labor for years to write one book.

_____

_____

_____

9. Only seconds after Letitia's audition had begun, the director said, "That will *suffice*." Fifteen notes were all he needed to hear to determine that she could not carry a tune.

_____

_____

_____

10. Following the enormous Thanksgiving feast, the guests dozed by the fire. The *surfeit* of food had left them as lethargic as hibernating bears.

_____

_____

_____

Name _____

Applying Meaning

Each question below contains a vocabulary word from this lesson. Answer each question "yes" or "no" in the space provided.

1. If you had difficulty finding a salesperson to wait on you, would you consider the personnel to be *officious?*

2. Are public displays of *affectation* illegal in some cultures?

3. Would an art student who painted three times as many paintings as her classmates in the same time period be considered *prolific?*

4. If a homeowner needs a watchdog, will a stuffed animal *suffice?*

5. If you are trying to lose weight, are you interested in the *efficacy* of a particular exercise regimen?

1. _____

2. _____

3. _____

4. _____

5. _____

For each question you answered "no," write a sentence using the vocabulary word correctly.

_____

_____

_____

_____

_____

_____

_____

_____

_____

_____

Write each sentence below. In the space write a form of the word in parentheses. The form of the word in parentheses may be correct.

6. The _____ silk roses were so beautiful that you had to smell them in order to differentiate between them and those grown in the garden. (factitious)

_____

_____

_____

7. Both the House and the Senate have spent long hours debating the _____ of universal health coverage. (feasible)

_____

_____

_____

8. Many colleges administer entrance examinations designed to test students' _____ in foreign languages and English. (proficient)

_____

_____

_____

9. With great _____ , the chef tossed the crepe from the pan, filled it with spiced bananas, topped it with a scoop of ice cream, and served it with a flourish. (facility or facileness)

_____

_____

_____

10. After only one week at her new job as a travel agent, Ms. DeMeo felt overwhelmed by the _____ of travelers. (surfeit)

_____

_____

Our Living Language

The word *facsimile* comes from the root *-fac-* and more specifically from the Latin phrase *fac simile,* meaning "make similar." Initially, the word meant "an exact copy." Today, the definition has been extended to include "a method of transmitting images or printed matter by electronic means," and the word is often shortened to *fax.*

Investigate Clipped Words: Use a dictionary and an encyclopedia of word origins to research the shortened, or clipped, words below. Then write a brief report on each word, and include a word history, a definition, and a sentence that illustrates the meaning of the word.

perk   hype   psych   still (n.)   **repo   retro**

How well do you remember the words you studied in Lessons 10 through 12? Take the following test covering the words from the last three lessons.

Part 1 Antonyms

Each question below includes a word in capital letters, followed by four words or phrases. Choose the word or phrase that is most nearly <u>opposite</u> in meaning to the word in capital letters. Consider all choices before deciding on your answer. Write the letter for your answer on the line provided.

Sample

| S. HIGH | (A) cold | (B) simple | S. _____C_____ |
| | (C) low | (D) foolish | |

1. FASTIDIOUS	(A) meticulous	(B) careless	1. _____
	(C) repulsive	(D) plodding	
2. INDOLENT	(A) unstable	(B) lazy	2. _____
	(C) industrious	(D) competent	
3. OFFICIOUS	(A) unauthorized	(B) courteous	3. _____
	(C) meddlesome	(D) restrained	
4. PROFICIENT	(A) incompetent	(B) adept	4. _____
	(C) extravagant	(D) insignificant	
5. SOPORIFIC	(A) invigorating	(B) experienced	5. _____
	(C) foolish	(D) sleep-inducing	
6. CELERITY	(A) good fortune	(B) slowness	6. _____
	(C) popularity	(D) dignitary	
7. QUIESCENT	(A) inactive	(B) uninterested	7. _____
	(C) perceptive	(D) boisterous	
8. SURFEIT	(A) contribution	(B) overabundance	8. _____
	(C) shortage	(D) replacement	
9. PRECLUDE	(A) foretell	(B) incorporate	9. _____
	(C) permit	(D) prevent	
10. REDOLENT	(A) essential	(B) odorless	10. _____
	(C) glowing	(D) likable	
11. ALACRITY	(A) hesitance	(B) liveliness	11. _____
	(C) obedience	(D) desperation	

Go on to next page. ➤

12. FACTITIOUS (A) artificial   (B) imaginary   12. _____

        (C) somber   (D) natural

13. PROLIFIC   (A) plentiful   (B) unproductive 13. _____

        (C) invisible   (D) unrewarding

14. RUSTIC   (A) corroded   (B) pastoral   14. _____

        (C) talented   (D) urban

15. ROMANTIC   (A) trustworthy (B) extravagant   15. _____

        (C) realistic   (D) nostalgic

Part 2 Matching Words and Meanings

Match the definition in Column B with the word in Column A.
Write the letter of the correct definition on the line provided.

Column A	Column B	
16. feasible	a. impressing favorably	16. _____
17. somnolence	b. effectiveness	17. _____
18. accoutrements	c. capable of being done	18. _____
19. prepossessing	d. limber	19. _____
20. ennui	e. original model	20. _____
21. facile	f. boredom	21. _____
22. efficacy	g. sleepiness	22. _____
23. prototype	h. diligent; hardworking	23. _____
24. lissome	i. easy; effortless	24. _____
25. sedulous	j. equipment or furnishings	25. _____

Name _____

Learning the Ropes

Rising several stories above the valley, the cliffs tower like **Gothic** cathe-
drals, seemingly as **impregnable** as a fortress. Yet, up close, these bluffs are
riven by cracks and punctuated with ledges and other irregularities that
aid rock climbers in their vertical journeys.

5   Rock climbing has recently begun to emerge from its cult-like **insularity**
and is adopting the features of other popular sports—organized contests,
prize money, crowds of spectators, and even a computerized ranking of
the participants. In addition, rock climbers are a growing breed. The in-
stallation of climbing walls in gyms has allowed urbanite climbers—the
10   general population as well as the sport's **elite**—to work out in all kinds of
weather. But it is only outdoors that they develop an appreciation and
reverence for the sport and the wilderness in which it takes place.

    Rock climbing's **mystique** has always been enhanced by the perception of
danger. While statistics are hard to come by, climbing is probably no more
15   dangerous than other thrill sports like hang-gliding and white-water raft-
ing. Deaths are rare, but because beginners can be overconfident, experts
exhort them to wear helmets and use a system of ropes and anchors to
ensure their safety.

    People climb for **sundry** reasons. Parents climb with their children to
20   strengthen family ties through shared participation and challenge. Some
people take to the cliffs as a form of escape or healing, while others are
motivated to overcome fears that are interfering with personal or career
development. Most new climbers, however, simply want to have fun and
learn a skill that will take them deeper into the wilderness and higher into
25   the mountains.

    Getting to the summit has never been the object of the sport. Although it
is rooted in mountaineering, where reaching the top *is* the goal, rock
climbing is a simple refinement. Its top athletes climb the same cliffs over
and over, striving to scale them by ever more difficult means. Other than
30   that, the rewards are personal. Coupled with the sense of well-being that
comes from meeting physical challenges, there is the thrill that results
from standing toe-to-toe with the **primal** emotion of fear and finding the
inner strength to move past it. The value of the climbing experience is not
measured by the technical grade or by the height of the climb. It comes
35   from the climber's relationship with the natural world, the intimacy of a
shared experience, and the discoveries made along the rocky way.

Words
elite
exhort
Gothic
impregnable
insularity
mystique
primal
reverence
rive
sundry

Each word in this lesson's word list appears in dark type in the selection you just read. Think about how the vocabulary word is used in the selection, then write the letter for the best answer to each question.

1. Which word or words could best replace *Gothic* in line 1?   1. _____
   (A) easily built   (B) of an architectural style employing
                                    pointed arches and steep roofs
   (C) unprincipled   (D) unimpressive

2. Something that is *impregnable* (line 2) can best be explained as   2. _____
   _____ .
   (A) delicate or flimsy   (B) clumsy
   (C) described in vivid detail (D) unconquerable

3. Which word or words could best replace *riven* in line 3?   3. _____
   (A) broken   (B) touched lightly
   (C) searched uncertainly   (D) cheated

4. *Insularity* (line 5) can best be explained as _____.   4. _____
   (A) environment   (B) isolation
   (C) destructive elements   (D) publicity

5. Which word or words could best replace *elite* in line 10?   5. _____
   (A) unskilled participants (B) announcers
   (C) people without knowledge (D) a group's best members

6. *Reverence* (line 12) can best be explained as _____.   6. _____
   (A) spite   (B) honor and respect
   (C) request on behalf of another (D) complexity

7. *Mystique* (line 13) can best be described as _____.   7. _____
   (A) an air of mystery and power (B) an exciting display
   (C) expectation   (D) knowledge and skill

8. Which word or words could best replace *exhort* in line 17?   8. _____
   (A) urge strongly   (B) discourage
   (C) embarrass   (D) trick

9. Which word could best replace *sundry* in line 19?   9. _____
   (A) stately   (B) mysterious
   (C) gloomy   (D) various

10. Which word or words could best replace *primal* in line 32?   10. _____
    (A) confined or restricted (B) comforting
    (C) primitive   (D) extending a great distance

Applying Meaning

Follow the directions below to write a sentence using a vocabulary word.

1. Describe an unusual character in a movie, television show, or book.
    Use the word *mystique.*

    _____

    _____

    _____

2. Describe something that has been damaged by a severe storm. Use
    any form of the word *rive.*

    _____

    _____

    _____

3. Describe how a person might show honor and respect for a country's
    leader. Use any form of the word *reverence.*

    _____

    _____

    _____

4. Explain how isolation affects a group of people. Use any form of the
    word *insularity.*

    _____

    _____

    _____

5. Use any form of the word *impregnable* in a sentence about a castle or
    fortress.

    _____

    _____

    _____

Each question below contains a vocabulary word from this lesson. Answer each question "yes" or "no" in the space provided.

6. Could a person have *sundry* reasons for making a particular career choice?

6. _____

7. Would someone who knows how to cook only hot dogs and beans be part of the *elite* of the Cooking Club?

7. _____

8. Would a doctor *exhort* her patient to exercise regularly and give up smoking?

8. _____

9. Is swimming a *primal* need for most people?

9. _____

10. If an architect were designing a warehouse, would he be likely to choose a *Gothic* style?

10. _____

For each question you answered "no," write a sentence using the vocabulary word correctly.

_____

_____

_____

_____

_____

_____

_____

_____

_____

_____

_____

Mastering Meaning

Imagine that you have just tried rock climbing or another exciting sport for the first time, and you are eager for a friend in another town to try it. Write a letter to your friend about the sport and your initial experiences with it. Make your letter as descriptive as possible. Use some of the words you studied in this lesson.

Name _____

Does it seem that every time you open a newspaper or flip on the television, some new disaster has befallen a country, a group, or an individual? Unfortunately, our world is full of problems, big and small. This lesson will give you ten words related to harm and injury.

Unlocking Meaning

Words
bestial حیوانی
canker نژدی،آت کامی
effete فرسوده،ازکارافتاده
heinous شنیع،نا گوار،بد
odious نفرت انگیز،کراهت آور
offal اشغال،لاشه،نخاله
perverse منحرف،گمراه
predatory شکارچی،شکارگر،غارتگر
sordid پست،فرومایه،بدجنس
vitiation تباهی،فساد

Read the sentences or short passages below. Write the letter for the correct definition of the italicized vocabulary word.

Abusing an elderly person is considered a sign of a *bestial* mentality.

1. ✓(A) brutal
   (B) weak
   (C) conservative
   (D) generous

The mayor announced the theme of his campaign: Violence is the *canker* in our society.

2. (A) incorrect assumption
   (B) overemphasized problem
   (C) acceptable norm
   ✓(D) source of spreading decay

Some political scientists argue that Britain is an *effete* society because, although once a world power, it is no longer a force in world politics.

3. (A) mighty
   ✓(B) depleted of effectiveness
   (C) compartmentalized
   (D) deprived of leadership

The death of innocent children is the most *heinous* result of war.

4. ✓(A) causing disgust and hatred
   (B) political
   (C) imposingly large
   (D) original

The dictator's *odious* treatment of minorities led to his overthrow.

5. (A) routine or standard
   (B) unnoticeable
   ✓(C) arousing strong dislike or intense displeasure
   (D) comical

1. _____

2. _____

3. _____

4. _____

5. _____

Seagulls are attracted to *offal;* true scavengers, they spend hours searching for appealing tidbits.

    6. (A) soft mud or slime

    ✓ (B) waste or rubbish

    (C) favorable circumstances

    (D) tropical fruits

6. _____

Possessing a *perverse* sense of humor, Dana always cracked tasteless jokes.

    7. (A) capable of being shaped or formed

    (B) widely appreciated

    (C) highly commendable

    ✓ (D) wicked; turned away from what is right or good

7. _____

Janisse watched the guests at the buffet table like a *predatory* bird. I kept expecting her to swoop down and grab a shrimp from someone's plate.

    8. (A) troubling to peace of mind

    (B) punishing

    ✓ (C) living by preying on other animals

    (D) available for action

8. _____

Many of the novels of Charles Dickens are filled with *sordid* details about women and children forced to work long hours in factories.

    9. ✓ (A) wretched; miserable

    (B) essential

    (C) unrealistic

    (D) poorly explained

9. _____

Some researchers contend that violent TV programs lead to the *vitiation* of young children.

    10. (A) positive reactions

    ✓ (B) corruption

    (C) disinterest

    (D) illness

10. _____

Applying Meaning

Decide which word in parentheses best completes the sentence. Then write
the sentence, adding the missing word.

1. His experiment was _*vitiated*_ because he failed to pay attention to exact
measurements. (perverted; vitiated)

   His experiment was perverted because he failed to pay
   attention to exact measurements.

2. The use of the guillotine in public executions is evidence of the _*bestiality*_
of punishment during the French Revolution. (bestiality; vitiation)

   The use of the guillotine in public executions is evidence of the
   bestiality of punishment during the french Revolution.

3. Richard the Lion-Hearted institutionalized the _*odious*_ punishment of
tarring and feathering thieves. (odious; predatory)

   Richard the Lion-Hearted institutionalized the punishment of
   tarring and feathering thieves.

4. Two firefighters confessed to the _*heinous*_ crime of setting a series of
fatal fires to relieve their boredom. (heinous; effete)

   Two firefighters confessed to the heinous crime of setting a series of
   fatal fires to relieve their boredom.

5. Having previously confessed to the murder, Desjardins _*Preversely*_ defended
himself in court by claiming to be a notorious liar. (effetely; perversely)

   Having previously confessed to the murder, Desjardins preversely
   defended himself in court by claiming to be a notorious liar.

6. In Japan, a talking crow was arrested for using _*sordid*_ language in public but refused to answer police questions. (cankerous; sordid)

   _____

   _____

   _____

7. Critics of tabloid newspapers consider most of the sensationalized articles pure _____. (effeteness; offal)

offal

_____

_____

_____

8. "Black Bart" was a daring *Predator* _____ who robbed at least 29 stagecoaches between 1875 and 1883. (offal; predator)

_____

_____

_____

9. Gene has joined an organization that pledges to rid the country of the _____ of slum dwellings. (canker; vitiation)

Canker

_____

_____

_____

10. Corruption had turned the small town's police force into an *effete* organization. Because police officers were so busy lining their own pockets, they were not effective in fighting crime. (effete; odious)

_____

_____

_____

Cultural Literacy Note

The word *schlock*, which means "shoddy, cheaply made, or defective merchandise," was borrowed from the Yiddish language, a combination of Hebrew and German. It probably derives from the German word *schlag*, meaning "a blow," and suggests that the goods have been knocked around and damaged.

Use the Dictionary: The Yiddish language has contributed many colorful words to English. Find the pronunciations and definitions of the Yiddish words below, and use each word in an original sentence.

kibitzer   maven   megillah   mensch   meshuga

Name _____

The Latin word *gignere* means "to beget" or "to produce." Another Latin word, *genus*, means "kind," as in "that kind of book." It is related to the Greek word *genos*, meaning "race" or "kind." Both roots appear as *-gen-* in English words. The root *-gress-*, from the Latin word *gradi*, means "to go." The root *-tac-*, from the Latin word *tacere*, means "to be silent." The roots in this lesson provide vocabulary words you can use to express the diverse ideas of family or origins, movement, and silence.

Root	Meaning	English Word
-gen-	race, kind to produce	genealogy progenitor
-gress-	to go	regress
-tac-	to be silent	tacit

Words

egress	خروج ، خارج شدن
genealogy	شجره نامه، نسب، دودمان
genus	دسته، طبقه
germinal	نطفه ای، جنینی
ingress	ورودی ، اجازه ورود
progenitor	جد، اجداد
regress	پس رفت، پس روی
retrogression	برگشت
tacit	خاموش
taciturn	کم حرف، آرام

Unlocking Meaning

Write the vocabulary word that fits each clue below. Then say the word and write a short definition. Compare your definition and pronunciation with those given on the flash card.

1. This adjective comes from the Latin *taciturnus*. A parrot that refuses to talk might be called this.

    Taciturn : Habitually Untalkative,

    Implied by or inferred from actions or statements.

    _____

2. This noun is a kind of "tree" that some families like to draw.

    Genealogy : Study of family descent

    Chart or recorded history of the descent of a person

    or family an ancestor or ancestors.

3. This word begins with the prefix *re-*, meaning "back." As a verb, it is the opposite of "to mature."

    Regress: go back ; move backward

    Return to a previous, usually worse or less developed

    state.

4. This noun has a prefix that means "in." A sign reading "IN" marks the location of this.

    Ingress :

    Permission to enter in a place.

    or sign

5. This adjective comes from the Latin word *germen,* meaning "bud" or "embryo." If you have an idea at this stage, you may want to gather more information before you present it to others.

Germinal : In or pertaining to the earliest stage of development.

6. This noun has the prefix *pro-,* meaning "before." A great-grandparent could be called this.

Progenitor : An originator of a line of descent.

7. This two-syllable noun comes to us unchanged from Latin. Wolves and dogs belong to the same one, but cats do not.

Genus : A class of objects divided into subordinate or kind with common attributes.

8. This noun has a prefix meaning "backward." It could be applied to the condition of someone who once was independent and self-sufficient but now needs help performing even basic tasks.

Retrogression : To return to a previous and usually worse condition.

9. This word is always an adjective. When people agree on something without talking about it, they may have this kind of understanding about it.

Tacit : Not spoken

10. This word, which can be a noun or a verb, has a prefix that means "out of." It is a safety hazard to have only one of these in a room that holds hundreds of people.

Egress : The act of going out.

Applying Meaning

Read each sentence or short passage below. Write "correct" on the answer line if the vocabulary word has been used correctly. Write "incorrect" on the answer line if the vocabulary word has been used incorrectly.

1. Even in its *germinal* form, Gil's paper was well-organized. With some revisions the second draft would be even better.

   1. *Correct*

2. Delores was a firm believer in *genealogical* charts. She thought that by consulting the ones published in the daily newspaper, she could be prepared for any crisis.
   astrological

   2. *incorrect*

3. William Whipper, a "conductor" on the Underground Railroad, was the *progenitor* of a line of reformers. Several of his children and grandchildren were activists as well.

   3. *Correct*

4. The explorers were trapped, their path of *egress* blocked by fallen rocks.

   4. *Correct*

   She was Excited
5. *Taciturn* about her vacation to Belize, Maybelle loved to talk about the wonders of its jungle and coral reef.

   5. *incorrect*

   genious
6. Albert Einstein is considered a scientific *genus*, due in part to his theory of relativity.

   6. *incorrect*

7. Some Third World nations in Africa, Asia, and South America are considered to be *retrogressive* because of their rapidly developing economies. *Progressive*

   7. *incorrect*

8. Some young children *regress* to thumb-sucking, bed-wetting, and other infantile behaviors when a sibling is born.

   8. *Correct*

9. Having discussed all of the consequences of skipping the final year of high school and starting college on an early admissions program, Jamie and her parents reached a *tacit* decision.
   Compromise

   9. *incorrect*

10. Most of the condominium residents used the garage as their means of *ingress*, leaving the front door for guests.

   10. *Correct*

For each word used incorrectly, write a sentence using the word properly.

_____

_____

_____

_____

_____

_____

_____

_____

_____

_____

_____

_____

_____

_____

_____

_____

_____

_____

_____

Our Living Language

One of the meanings of the English word *general* is "a commissioned officer in the United States Army, Air Force, or Marine Corps, ranking above lieutenant general." The word comes from the Latin adjective *generalis,* which literally means "pertaining to the whole genus, kind, or class." A general's responsibility is to command a whole military force, be it a brigade or an entire army.

Research Military Ranks: Use a dictionary or an etymological encyclopedia to do some research about the military ranks listed below. Then make a chart of these ranks that includes each word's derivation, the derivation's connection to the English word, and a definition.

corporal   sergeant   brigadier   captain   lieutenant

Name _____

How well do you remember the words you studied in Lessons 13 through 15? Take the following test covering the words from the last three lessons.

Part 1 Choose the Correct Meaning

Each question below includes a word in capital letters, followed by four words or phrases. Choose the word or phrase that is <u>closest</u> in meaning to the word in capital letters. Write the letter for your answer on the line provided.

Sample

S. FINISH	(A) enjoy	(B) complete	S. ___B___
	(C) destroy	(D) enlarge	

1. EFFETE	(A) practical	(B) dazzling	1. _C_
	✓(C) exhausted	(D) vigorous	

2. ODIOUS	(A) foul-smelling	✓(B) offensive	2. _B_
	(C) apparent	(D) sensitive	

3. TACITURN	✓(A) not talkative	(B) tasteless	3. _A_
	(C) considerate	(D) fluent	

4. PROGENITOR	(A) forecast	(B) descendant	4. _C_
	✓(C) ancestor	(D) extension	

5. PRIMAL	✓(A) primitive	(B) modern	5. _A_
	(C) essential	(D) powerful	

6. BESTIAL	(A) reasonable	(B) strong	6. _D_
	(C) kindhearted	✓(D) brutal	

7. TACIT	(A) rude	✓(B) unexpressed	7. _B_
	(C) tawdry	(D) clever	

8. SORDID	(A) worrisome	(B) honorable	8. _D_
	(C) quiet	✓(D) wretched	

9. EGRESS	(A) lengthy speech	(B) female official	9. _C_
	✓(C) exit	(D) misleading remark	

10. SUNDRY	(A) same	(B) concise	10. _C_
	✓(C) various	(D) bright	

Go on to next page. ➤

11. HEINOUS   ✓(A) abominable   (B) disorderly   **11.** _A_

                      (C) glorious   (D) courageous

12. INGRESS   (A) appearance   ✓(B) entrance   **12.** _B_

                      (C) exit   (D) backward movement

13. PERVERSE   (A) morose   (B) observant   **13.** _D_

                      (C) bewildered   ✓(D) wicked

14. RIVE   (A) endanger   (B) anger   **14.** _D_

                      (C) enlarge   ✓(D) break apart

15. VITIATION   (A) religious journey (B) liveliness   **15.** _C_

                      ✓(C) corruption   (D) purification

Part 2 Matching Words and Meanings

Match the definition in Column B with the word in Column A.
Write the letter of the correct answer on the line provided.

Column A	Column B	
16. canker	✓a. revert	b **16.** _Source of decay_
17. genealogy	✓b. source of decay	f **17.** _family Tree_
18. offal	✓c. unconquerable	i **18.** _garbage; refuse_
19. insularity	✓d. in the earliest stage	e **19.** _isolation_
20. regress	✓e. isolation	a **20.** _revert_
21. predatory	✓f. family tree	h **21.** _Preying on other animals_
22. genus	✓g. urge strongly	j **22.** _class; kind; sort_
23. impregnable	✓h. preying on other animals	c **23.** _unconquerable_
24. germinal	✓i. garbage; refuse	d **24.** _in the earliest stage_
25. exhort	✓j. class; kind; sort	g **25.** _urge strongly_

Name _____

Three Laws That Must Be Obeyed

Sir Isaac Newton (1642–1727), a British physicist and mathematician, possessed one of the keenest scientific intellects of his time. But in spite of his brilliance, he was a **humble** person who always tried to **depreciate** his contributions to science, preferring instead to honor the scientists who

5 had preceded him. He once remarked, "If I have seen further [than others], it is by standing upon the shoulders of Giants."

Newton is famous primarily for his laws describing motion. When the plague forced Cambridge University to shut down temporarily, Newton left the university and stayed for a time at his mother's farm. Instead of

10 **dallying**, however, Newton used this **respite** from his formal education to study and think. It was during this period that Newton formulated the three laws of motion that bear his name. These three laws reduce nearly all the motion we observe to concepts that are **relatively** simple, considering the complexities of physics.

15 There is a popular, but no doubt **apocryphal**, story that Newton discovered gravity when an apple fell on his head as he sat under a tree. While there is no evidence to support this particular story, it seems certain that observing falling objects caused Newton to think about the forces at work in the universe. Newton's First Law contradicted the popular belief that

20 it was natural for moving objects to slow down and eventually stop moving. Instead Newton stated that any change in the motion of an object was the result of a force. A ball or brick set in motion slows down and stops because of the force of friction. If a frictionless environment were available, a moving object could theoretically stay in motion forever. Newton's

25 First Law is **reinforced** whenever objects are sent into the almost frictionless environment of space.

Newton's Second Law describes acceleration, or changes in speed. Newton found that acceleration is directly proportional to the amount of force applied and inversely proportional to mass. To **paraphrase** this law, if an ob-

30 ject is pushed twice as hard it will accelerate twice as much. If you double its mass, and push it with the same force, it will accelerate by just half as much. This law is important to engineers today as they work to increase the efficiency of automobiles. One of the principal methods for increasing gas mileage is reducing the mass of the vehicle. Thus, the hulking **behemoths**

35 of a few years ago have been replaced by the **svelte** sport sedans of today.

Perhaps because of its **brevity**, Newton's Third Law is one of the most quoted: For every action there is an equal and opposite reaction. If you step off a boat that is not securely moored, the boat may move backward as much as you try to move forward. If your goal was to step on the dock,

40 Newton's Third Law could leave you very wet.

Words

- apocryphal
- behemoth
- brevity
- dally
- depreciate
- paraphrase
- reinforce
- relatively
- respite
- svelte

Each word in this lesson's word list appears in dark type in the selection you just read. Think about how the vocabulary word is used in the selection, then write the letter for the best answer to each question.

1. Which word or words could best replace *depreciate* in line 3?
   ✓(A) lessen the value of   (B) exaggerate
   (C) publish   (D) advertise

   1. _____

2. Which words could best replace *dallying* in line 10?
   (A) doing research   ✓(B) wasting time
   (C) making arrangements   (D) making empty promises

   2. _____

3. A *respite* (line 10) can best be described as _____.
   (A) an acceleration   (B) a narrow escape
   ✓(C) a period of rest   (D) an intense hatred

   3. _____

4. Which word could best replace *relatively* in line 13?
   (A) overly   (B) never
   (C) mysteriously   ✓(D) comparatively

   4. _____

5. An *apocryphal* (line 15) story is one that is _____.
   ✓(A) probably untrue   (B) often retold
   (C) written in another language (D) highly complicated

   5. _____

6. Which word or words could best replace *reinforced* in line 25?
   (A) denied   ✓(B) made stronger
   (C) challenged   (D) ignored

   6. _____

7. Which word or words could best replace *paraphrase* in line 29?
   (A) disprove   ✓(B) restate more simply
   (C) release from captivity   (D) request a change in

   7. _____

8. A *behemoth* (line 34) is _____.
   (A) a legendary city   (B) a type of mineral
   (C) an unreliable machine   ✓(D) something enormous

   8. _____

9. Which word or words could best replace *svelte* in line 35?
   ✓(A) slender or graceful   (B) unpopular
   (C) heavy   (D) imaginary

   9. _____

10. Which word or words could best replace *brevity* in line 36?
    (A) delightful rhythm   (B) sense of superiority
    ✓(C) shortness   (D) immoral conclusion

    10. _____

Applying Meaning

Follow the directions below to write a sentence using a vocabulary word.

1. Use *apocryphal* in a sentence about a famous hero.

_____

_____

_____

2. Use any form of the word *depreciate* in a sentence about an outstanding athlete.

_____

_____

_____

3. Compare the size or weight of two things, using the word *relatively*.

_____

_____

_____

4. Use any form of the word *respite* to describe something you did last summer.

_____

_____

_____

5. Use the word *svelte* to describe a dancer or athlete.

_____

_____

_____

6. Describe how you would support your arguments in a debate or a paper. Use any form of the word *reinforce*.

_____

_____

_____

Each question below contains at least one vocabulary word from this lesson. Answer each question "yes" or "no" in the space provided.

7. Could someone *paraphrase* an article for the sake of *brevity*?

7. _____

8. Is it wise to *dally* as a way of preparing for an important examination?

8. _____

9. Is a butterfly a *behemoth*?

9. _____

10. When people are angry, do they sometimes do things out of *respite*?

10. _____

For each word used incorrectly, write a sentence using the word properly.

_____

_____

_____

_____

_____

_____

_____

_____

_____

_____

_____

_____

_____

_____

Mastering Meaning

Isaac Newton lived before the invention of the automobile. However, one of today's most important automotive safety devices — the seat belt — is a direct application of Newton's First Law. Using as many words from this lesson as you can, write an advertisement featuring Sir Isaac explaining why today's drivers need to use seat belts.

Name _____

Of what do you strongly disapprove? Would you protest against United States involvement in the wars of other countries? Would you condemn a friend who cheated in school? The words in this lesson all concern negative opinions and ways of expressing them.

Unlocking Meaning

Read the sentences or short passages below. Write the letter for the correct definition of the italicized vocabulary word.

In 1972, a pickpocket who was *adjudged* guilty for stealing $15.11 from a woman's purse was ordered to wear enormous woolen mittens whenever he appeared in public for the next two years.

1. (A) damaged by underhanded means
   ✓(B) determined by legal procedure
   (C) suspected
   (D) provoked or teased

When my brother absent-mindedly answered the telephone with "Yeah?" Aunt Margaret *berated* him for his poor manners.

2. (A) laughed at
   (B) cheered
   (C) rewarded
   ✓(D) scolded angrily and at length

It was Horace Fletcher's firmly held conviction that we chew too little and therefore do not get the full nutritional value of our food. This belief no doubt led him to compose the motto "Nature will *castigate* those who don't masticate."

3. ✓(A) severely punish
   (B) highlight
   (C) appreciate
   (D) make use of

Noah *chided* his Siberian husky when she jumped onto the couch. The puppy was beginning to respond to the words "bad dog."

4. (A) treated with courteous attention
   (B) looked after with care
   ✓(C) scolded mildly
   (D) kept down by use of force

Words

adjudge	سرزنش کردن، معلوم کردن، داوری کردن
berate	سرزنش کردن
castigate	تنبیه کردن، شدید آنتقاد کردن
chide	سرزنش کردن، گله کردن
disparage	انکار کردن، ثقلت، عیب، چیزی
insinuation	بی لحاظ کردن / زنایی، ایما، رمز، طعنه
philippic	سخنرانی تند و آتشکای
stricture	خشونت، سخت گیری
supercilious	مغرور، ازروی غرور و علو
tirade	سخنرانی دراز و شدید اللحن

1. _____

2. _____

3. _____

4. _____

Although many people *disparaged* Marc Chagall's habit of paying for even small purchases with personal checks, the artist always had a healthy bank balance. Most merchants failed to cash his checks, figuring that his signature would make the checks valuable collector's items.

5. (A) belittled
   (B) raised to a higher moral ground
   (C) omitted from consideration
   (D) deprived of strength

5. _____

"I resent your *insinuation,* sir," huffed the marquis. "Either call me a cheater to my face, or drop the issue entirely."

6. (A) wasteful action
   (B) uncontrolled fit
   (C) accumulation of miscellaneous things
   (D) slyly indirect suggestion

6. _____

Testifying before a televised session of the committee, the physician delivered a *philippic* against the tobacco industry.

7. (A) prescription
   (B) bitter condemnation
   (C) list of ingredients
   (D) unusual object

7. _____

In 1843 a former slave named Isabella took the name Sojourner Truth and began to speak out against the *strictures* that had been placed on African Americans' freedom.

8. (A) labor without pay
   (B) lists of tasks
   (C) restrictions
   (D) inevitable ruin

8. _____

Many traditional musicians regard Harry Partch with a *supercilious* attitude. It was not enough for Partch to abandon the twelve-tone scale and invent his own forty-three-interval octave; he also found it necessary to invent and build his own musical instruments.

9. (A) haughty
   (B) contagious
   (C) designed for two purposes
   (D) tedious

9. _____

During the Victorian era, the writer of an etiquette book actually delivered an hour-long *tirade* to librarians about the proper way to shelve books: alphabetical order should prevail, but books by male and female authors should never be placed side by side.

10. (A) computer program
    (B) concert
    (C) videotape
    (D) long, angry speech

10. _____

Applying Meaning

Decide which word in parentheses best completes the sentence. Then write the sentence, adding the missing word.

1. With a(n) _____ shrug of her shoulders, Gwen strode out the door, ignoring the pleas of her less competitive teammates. (insinuating; supercilious)

   _____

   _____

   _____

2. The accused man was _____ mentally incompetent to stand trial. (adjudged; chided)

   _____

   _____

   _____

3. After three hours of practice, the coach _____ the players for their inability to execute the play. (castigated; insinuated)

   _____

   _____

   _____

4. My dad's _____ remarks about my girlfriend are annoying. Why doesn't he just come out and say he doesn't like her? (adjudging; insinuating)

   _____

   _____

   _____

5. Ashamed of losing his temper but unable to admit it, Tomas turned his anger on his younger brothers and _____ them for their noisiness and lack of discipline. (adjudged; berated)

   _____

   _____

   _____

6. The _____ the teacher placed on her students made it difficult for them to complete their papers on time. (disparagements; strictures)

   _____

   _____

   _____

7. Rani did not mean to _____ the potter's work, but she was surprised at the uneven forms and the careless glazing. (chide; disparage)

   _____

   _____

   _____

8. The principal's _____ focused on the lack of team spirit; for almost an hour, he criticized our lack of responsibility and our selfishness. (stricture; philippic)

   _____

   _____

   _____

9. Following the principal's speech, the coaches had their own _____ to deliver; for another forty minutes we heard how apathetic we are. (strictures; tirades)

   _____

   _____

   _____

10. When the toddler ran toward the street, the babysitter gently took her by the hand and _____ her in a soft voice. (chided; berated)

    _____

    _____

    _____

Our Living Language

Philippic, one of the words in this lesson, has a rather interesting history. Philip II of Macedon (382–336 B.C.) was an ambitious ruler and military genius who attempted to take over Greece state by state. After Philip's armies won numerous victories, an eloquent Athenian orator named Demosthenes delivered a series of three passionate speeches against the Macedonian monarch's plan to annex Athens to his kingdom. These speeches, called the Philippics, defended Greek liberty and took their name from the object of their anger.

Write a Report: Many English words come from the names of famous Greek and Roman people and places. Use a dictionary and other library resources to research the origins and definitions of one of the words below. Then write your findings in a report.

| stoic | epicurean | Socratic | Platonic | Spartan |

Name _____

The root *-cred-* comes from the Latin word *credere*, meaning "to believe."
The root *-fid-* comes from the Latin word *fidere*, meaning "to trust." When combined with a variety of prefixes and suffixes, these roots contribute many words to our language. You will learn ten of them in this lesson.

Root	Meaning	English Word
-cred-	to believe	credence
-fid-	to trust	perfidious

Unlocking Meaning

Write the vocabulary word that fits each clue below. Then say the word and write a short definition. Compare your definition and pronunciation with those given on the flash card.

1. This noun comes from the Latin word *affidare*, meaning "to pledge." If you are a witness to a traffic accident, you may have to sign this in the presence of a judge.

   affidavit _____

   _____

   _____

2. This noun or adjective comes from the Latin *fiducia*. A person who is a guardian often acts in this capacity.

   fiduciary _____

   _____

   _____

3. This adjective has a prefix that is a form of *dis-*, meaning "absence of." This kind of person lacks faith in himself or herself.

   diffident _____

   _____

   _____

4. This adjective has a suffix meaning "possessing" or "full of." If you are this kind of person, you can easily be tricked.

   credulous _____

   _____

   _____

Words

affidavit اقرارنامه، سوگندنامه

credence اعتقاد، باور، اعتماد

credibility باور پذیری، باورکردنی

credulous زودباور، ساده لوح

diffident بدون اعتماد بنفس

fealty وفاداری، وظیفه شناسی

fiduciary امانی

miscreant بدجنس، پست

perfidious بی وفا، نیرنگ خائن

recreant ترسو، بزدل، خائن

5. This adjective has the prefix *per-*, meaning "through." Benedict Arnold and Judas were this.

Perfidious

6. This noun from the Latin word *fidelitas* is what the President swears upon taking the oath of office.

fealty

7. This two-syllable noun has a suffix meaning "state" or "condition." Believing gossip is giving it this.

credence

8. This noun or adjective has the prefix *mis-*, meaning "wrong" or "bad." This kind of person in old Westerns always had a mustache and wore a black hat.

Miscreant

9. This noun has a suffix meaning "ability" or "suitability." People who lie all the time lack this.

credibility

10. This noun or adjective has the prefix *re-*, meaning "backward" or "back." The lion in *The Wizard of Oz* was accused of being this.

recreant

Applying Meaning

Decide which word in parentheses best completes the sentence. Then write the sentence, adding the missing word.

1. The expert witness signed a(n) _____ that contained her testimony about the breach of legal ethics. (affidavit; fealty)

   _____

   _____

   _____

2. As an officer of the condominium board of directors, Ms. Bergman had the _____ responsibility to inform the owners of changes in the association's bylaws. (fiduciary; perfidious)

   _____

   _____

   _____

3. The presence of large quantities of sulfur gives _____ to the accusation that oil refineries are polluting the water. (credence; diffidence)

   _____

   _____

   _____

4. At a White House dinner, General Winfield Scott had a wallet stolen from his pocket; the _____ was never apprehended.
   (credibility; miscreant)

   _____

   _____

   _____

5. During the Vietnam War, those who fled to Canada or used other means to avoid the draft were considered by some to be _____.
   (fiduciaries; recreants)

   _____

   _____

   _____

Each question below contains a vocabulary word from this lesson. Answer each question "yes" or "no" in the space provided.

6. Would a textbook that contained numerous factual errors lack *credibility*? 6. No

7. Would a *perfidious* person be a loyal friend? 7. No

8. Is *fealty* a characteristic of traitors? 8. No

9. Would a *credulous* person believe a story in the tabloids claiming that Elvis is still alive? 9. Yes

10. Is a *diffident* person likely to audition for the leading role in a school play? 10. No

For each question you answered "no," write a sentence using the vocabulary word correctly.

_____

_____

_____

_____

_____

_____

_____

_____

_____

_____

Test-Taking Strategies

Tests of vocabulary sometimes ask you to choose a synonym, a word that has the same or nearly the same meaning, for the word being tested. You are usually given four or five choices from which to select the correct synonym. Look at each choice and eliminate any answers that are clearly wrong. Test makers may try to confuse you by including words with sounds and spellings similar to the correct word's or by including antonyms, words with opposite meanings, among the choices.

Practice: Choose the <u>synonym</u> for the word in capital letters. Write your choice on the answer line.

1. CAPTIVATING (A) humorous (B) enchanting 1. _____
   (C) innocent (D) suspicious

2. ASCEND (A) protect (B) decide 2. _____
   (C) recover (D) climb

3. CONTROVERSY (A) crime (B) scream 3. _____
   (C) conflict (D) danger

Name _____

How well do you remember the words you studied in Lessons 16 through 18? Take the following test covering the words from the last three lessons.

Part 1 Antonyms

Each question below includes a word in capital letters, followed by four words or phrases. Choose the word or phrase that is most nearly <u>opposite</u> in meaning to the word in capital letters. Consider all choices before deciding on your answer. Write the letter for your answer on the line provided.

Sample

S. HIGH	(A) cold	(B) simple	S. _____ C _____
	(C) low	(D) foolish	

1. FEALTY — (A) dread — (B) faithfulness — ✓(D) disloyalty — (C) probability — 1. _____

2. CHIDE — (A) scold — ✓(B) praise — (C) revere — (D) discourage — 2. _____

3. BREVITY — ✓(A) lengthiness — (B) permanence — (C) terseness — (D) sluggishness — 3. _____

4. PERFIDIOUS — (A) treacherous — (B) orderly — ✓(C) loyal — (D) careful — 4. _____

5. SUPERCILIOUS — (A) analytical — ✓(B) humble — (C) important — (D) cheerful — 5. _____

6. DEPRECIATE — (A) forgive — (B) organize — (C) prolong — ✓(D) enhance — 6. _____

7. REINFORCE — (A) modernize — (B) compensate — ✓(C) weaken — (D) strengthen — 7. _____

8. CASTIGATE — ✓(A) praise — (B) criticize — (C) confine — (D) listen — 8. _____

9. CREDULOUS — (A) foolish — (B) surprised — (C) honorable — ✓(D) doubting — 9. _____

10. RECREANT — (A) gracious — (B) exhausted — (C) uncivilized — ✓(D) brave — 10. _____

Go on to next page. ➤

11. SVELTE   ✓(A) bulky   (B) slender   11. _____

    (C) graceful   (D) lanky

12. BERATE   (A) mourn   (B) implore   12. _____

    ✓(C) compliment   (D) humiliate

13. CREDENCE   (A) acceptance   (B) confidence   13. _____

    ✓(C) disbelief   (D) disenchantment

14. MISCREANT   (A) thief   (B) slanderous remark   14. _____

    (C) careful plan   ✓(D) hero

15. DIFFIDENT   (A) industrious   ✓(B) self-confident   15. _____

    (C) scornful   (D) identical

Part 2 Matching Words and Meanings

Match the definition in Column B with the word in Column A. Write the letter of the correct definition on the line provided.

Column A	Column B	
16. behemoth	a. written statement made under oath	16. _b._
17. disparage	b. something huge in size or power	17. _g._
18. credibility	c. waste time	18. _d._
19. respite	d. believability	19. _j._
20. affidavit	e. restriction	20. _a._
21. tirade	f. indirect suggestion	21. _i._
22. stricture	g. belittle	22. _e._
23. dally	h. restate more simply	23. _c._
24. insinuation	i. long, angry speech	24. _f._
25. paraphrase	j. short period of rest	25. _h._

Name _____

Maya Lin's Architecture of Remembrance

Maya Lin is an architect whose public monuments have helped countless people come to terms with some painful aspects of U.S. history. Both the Vietnam Veterans Memorial in Washington, D.C., and the Civil Rights Memorial in Montgomery, Alabama, have become places of healing, pro-
5 viding **solace** to those who are moved by their **spare**, sculptural simplicity.

The Vietnam Memorial consists of two long, low black granite walls built into the earth in a wide V shape. The highly polished stone, on which the names of some 58,000 veterans are **incised** in the order that they died or disappeared, also serves as a kind of mirror, reflecting the images of visi-
10 tors. In spite of its beauty, Lin's design involved her in an **imbroglio** that illustrated the dissension created by the Vietnam War. Some veterans resented that the work of a Chinese American had been chosen, while others derogatorily referred to the monument as a "degrading ditch" or a "wall of shame." During the dedication ceremony for the memorial, Maya
15 Lin's name was never mentioned.

Lin was later asked by the Southern Poverty Law Center to design a memorial to those who have died in the struggle for racial equality. Since it was largely the speeches of Martin Luther King Jr. that had served to **edify** participants in the civil rights movement, Lin chose as her theme a line
20 from his celebrated "I Have a Dream" speech: ". . . until justice rolls down like waters and righteousness like a mighty stream." The Civil Rights Memorial is composed of two separate but related structures. The first is a black granite disk that rests on an **asymmetrical** column so that it appears to be floating. Around its perimeter are inscribed 53 chronological
25 events in the history of the civil rights movement and the names of 40 people who lost their lives in the struggle. The second component is a nine-foot-high wall with King's words engraved into its surface. Water spills down the wall and flows gently through a hole in the disk.

Lin sees the contemplative, **intuitive** spirit of both of these public monu-
30 ments as distinctly Asian. Unlike what she considers the **didactic** bent of Western art, her purpose is not to instruct, but to let viewers make their own interpretations.

Although Maya Lin has designed homes, a park, and a sculptural ceiling for New York City's Pennsylvania Station, she currently concentrates on
35 more personal works. In small-scale sculptures, she shapes lead, which she favors because it is **supple**, with bits of broken glass. In some of her more recent pieces mottled beeswax is combined with lead to form a **striated** pattern. Like her public works, these sculptures possess an emotional and psychological context that demands viewer participation.

Words

asymmetrical

didactic

edify

imbroglio

incise

intuitive

solace

spare

striate

supple

Each word in this lesson's word list appears in dark type in the selection you just read. Think about how the vocabulary word is used in the selection, then write the letter for the best answer to each question.

1. *Solace* (line 5) can best be explained as _____.
   (A) a source of revenue
   (B) a strong craving
   (C) sudden impairment of function
   (D) comfort in sorrow or misfortune

   1. _____

2. Which word or words could best replace *spare* in line 5?
   (A) musical
   (B) not lavish; lean
   (C) demanding great effort
   (D) insincere

   2. _____

3. Which word or words could best replace *incised* in line 8?
   (A) spread damaging charges against
   (B) related to a cause or source
   (C) reduced
   (D) engraved

   3. _____

4. An *imbroglio* (line 10) can best be explained as a(n) _____.
   (A) complicated situation
   (B) art object
   (C) romantic poem or song
   (D) careless mistake

   4. _____

5. Which word or words could best replace *edify* in line 18?
   (A) instruct morally or spiritually
   (B) identify
   (C) arrest and imprison
   (D) disband

   5. _____

6. Something that is *asymmetrical* (line 23) can best be explained as _____.
   (A) natural
   (B) ancient Greek
   (C) lacking balanced proportions
   (D) shapeless

   6. _____

7. Which word or words could best replace *intuitive* in line 29?
   (A) uncivilized
   (B) sensing without rational thought
   (C) miniature
   (D) marked by delicate ornamentation

   7. _____

8. Something that is *didactic* (line 30) can best be explained as _____.
   (A) that which can be endured
   (B) radiant
   (C) very disagreeable
   (D) intended to instruct

   8. _____

9. Which word or words can best replace *supple* in line 36?
   (A) charitable
   (B) easily bent
   (C) very costly
   (D) intense

   9. _____

10. Something that is *striated* (line 37) can best be described as _____.
    (A) unattractive
    (B) casual
    (C) striped or ridged
    (D) trivial

    10. _____

Applying Meaning

Write each sentence below. In the space write a form of the word in parentheses. The form of the word in parentheses may be correct.

1. The antique ring and matching bracelet were _____ with a design of leaves and flowers surrounding decorative initials. (incise)

   _____

   _____

   _____

2. As Tony awakened to brilliant sunshine, he knew _____ that today was the day that he would receive the long-awaited letter. (intuitive)

   _____

   _____

   _____

3. The minister chose a reading from the New Testament to _____ his parishioners. (edify)

   _____

   _____

   _____

4. Unlike her grandmother, Rosa preferred to arrange the knickknacks over her fireplace _____, with a tall vase on one side and several short candleholders on the other. (asymmetrical)

   _____

   _____

   _____

5. The pottery bowl was pure white except for several deep _____ of grey-green around the top. (striate)

   _____

   _____

   _____

6. After her husband died, Ms. Kougias found _____ in her volunteer work at the hospital. (solace)

_____

_____

_____

7. Having moved seven times in the last ten years, the LeFays have managed to keep their furnishings _____. (spare)

_____

_____

_____

8. Randi loves the _____ of her new leather handbag. (supple)

_____

_____

_____

9. Some readers like the _____ of Aesop's fables; each one has a moral lesson. (didactic)

_____

_____

_____

10. People who are chronic liars often find themselves in _____, unable to remember what they told to whom. (imbroglio)

_____

_____

_____

Mastering Meaning

Imagine that an organization has asked you to design a monument to commemorate an event in history or honor an important person. Think about the organization's values and goals; then choose a quotation as the inspiration for your memorial. Write a proposal that explains your choice and describes your design, including location, size, materials, and appearance. Use some of the words you studied in this lesson.

Name _____

Because of its long tradition of welcoming words from other languages, English has a particularly rich, flexible, and creative vocabulary. Throughout the history of the language, invasion, trade, exploration, colonization, and immigration offered ready access to a treasure trove of words and expressions. With borrowings from Latin, Greek, German, French, Spanish, and Italian, to name but a few, our language has countless borrowed words from which to choose.

Unlocking Meaning

Read the sentences or short passages below. Write the letter for the correct definition of the italicized vocabulary words.

When the superintendent decided that interactive multimedia should be introduced in all school computer labs, she appointed an *ad hoc* committee to research hardware and software alternatives and applications.

1. (A) concerned with a specific purpose
   (B) causing shock or horror
   (C) characterized by intelligence
   (D) splendid in appearance

Sheryl is so enthusiastic about her volunteer work that she often gets carried away, relating experience after experience *ad infinitum*.

2. (A) with hostility
   (B) noisily
   (C) without end
   (D) in clearly defined terms

A *cabal* of powerful stockholders devised a plan for replacing the corporation's president with someone they could more easily control.

3. (A) athletic team
   (B) group of secret plotters
   (C) political party
   (D) religious cult

During the 1960s the issue of the draft was a *cause célèbre*. The war in Vietnam divided people from all walks of life.

4. (A) small, secret group united for a common interest
   (B) place where two things connect
   (C) severe shortage
   (D) issue arousing widespread controversy

Words

ad hoc	دلهٔ خاص
ad infinitum	بی‌انتها
cabal	دزد ملک ، دسیسهٔ مرکزید
cause célèbre	
chutzpah	گستاخی
juggernaut	نیروی نیرومند سهیب
nabob	بولدار ، نایب السلطنه
persona non grata	فرد نامطلوب
quid pro quo	درعوض
shibboleth	آزمون هوش ملک
	امتحان
	اصطلاح بی‌بامعنا و متداول مردم

1. _____

2. _____

3. _____

4. _____

Only someone with a lot of *chutzpah* would tell Ms. Mitchell that the charity benefit she organized was a disaster.

5. (A) a range of values
   (B) brazen nerve; impudence
   (C) final mention
   (D) something that unites

5. _____

The *juggernaut* of public outrage over increasing violent crime caused the legislature to pass a new law banning assault weapons.

6. (A) tendency
   (B) suitable occasion
   (C) expected obstacle
   (D) overwhelming force

6. _____

My parents think sports stars are a bunch of *nabobs* who expect to be treated like some kind of royalty.

7. (A) timid individuals
   (B) heads of households
   (C) wealthy and prominent people
   (D) poor students

7. _____

After the attack on Pearl Harbor, the Japanese diplomat was *persona non grata* and given 24 hours to leave the United States.

8. (A) extremely ugly
   (B) not acceptable; unwelcome
   (C) careless and clumsy
   (D) satisfied

8. _____

The teacher agreed not to assign homework over the Thanksgiving holiday, but as a *quid pro quo* she insisted that every student help with the food drive.

9. (A) something given or received for something else
   (B) prolonged argument
   (C) sly trick
   (D) violent action

9. _____

The *shibboleth* "clean and green" is used by professional truck drivers to tell each other that a highway can be traveled at maximum speed.

10. (A) insulting remark
    (B) word or phrase associated with a particular group
    (C) original idea
    (D) unexpected behavior

10. _____

Applying Meaning

Each question below contains a vocabulary term from this lesson. Answer each question "yes" or "no" in the space provided.

1. Would it take *chutzpah* to break into the middle of a long line of people waiting to purchase movie tickets?

2. Would a *nabob* frequently need financial assistance from a relative?

3. Are your brothers and sisters your *shibboleths*?

4. Would a person who is smoking a cigarette be *persona non grata* at a meeting of the American Cancer Society?

5. Would the city council be considered an *ad hoc* governing body?

1. _Yes_

2. _No_

3. _No_

4. _Yes_

5. _No_

For each question you answered "no," write a sentence using the vocabulary term correctly.

_____

_____

_____

_____

_____

_____

_____

_____

_____

_____

Follow the directions below to write a sentence using a vocabulary term.

6. Explain an agreement between countries that requires compromises on both sides. Use the expression *quid pro quo*.

   Many years ago, Persia agreed to don't attack the Egypt and as a quid pro quo the Egypt sent some gift to persian kingdom.

7. Comment on an event or person in history. Use the word *juggernaut*.

   Her mother's death made a juggernaut pain in her life.

   _____

   _____

8. Describe someone who monopolizes a conversation. Use the expression *ad infinitum.*

_____

_____

_____

9. Comment on the efforts of a group interested in conserving the environment. Use the expression *cause célèbre.*

_____

_____

_____

10. Use *cabal* in a sentence about a real or imaginary conspiracy.

_____

_____

_____

Cultural Literacy Note

Four of the expressions in this lesson come directly from Latin: *ad hoc, ad infinitum, persona non grata,* and *quid pro quo.* Because Latin was once considered the universal language of learning, it is not surprising that many of our scholarly, technical, and legal terms and expressions come directly from Latin. What may be surprising, however, is the number of Latin expressions we use in the same way they were used in ancient Rome.

Cooperative Learning: Work with a partner to investigate the origins and definitions of the expressions below. Then write an "Applying Meaning" activity like the one that appears at the top of the previous page. Exchange your paper with another pair's paper to see if you and your partner can answer the "yes" or "no" questions correctly.

caveat emptor	mea culpa	
modus operandi	bona fide	sine qua non

Name _____

The roots *-vers-* and *-vert-*, from the Latin words *versare* and *vertere,* mean "to turn." With the addition of various prefixes and suffixes, these roots contribute many important words to English. For example, if you *divert* attention from yourself, you distract others or turn their notice elsewhere. If you know someone who is an *introvert,* that person has a tendency to turn inward. In this lesson you will learn other words that refer to the action or process of turning.

Root	Meaning	English Word
-vers-	to turn	aversion
-vert-		incontrovertible

Unlocking Meaning

Words
aversion
avert
inadvertent
incontrovertible
malversation
obverse
vertex
vertiginous
vertigo
vortex

A vocabulary word appears in italics in each sentence or short passage below. Find the root in the vocabulary word and think about how the word is used in the passage. Then write a definition for the vocabulary word. Compare your definition with the definition on the flash card.

1. If you had an *aversion* to snakes, you probably would not visit the reptile house at the zoo.

   _____

   _____

   _____

2. At a horror movie, you can *avert* your eyes or close them if you don't want to watch the scary parts.

   _____

   _____

   _____

3. If you accidentally overlook an item on a test, you have made an *inadvertent* error.

   _____

   _____

   _____

4. Since the witnesses provided *incontrovertible* evidence of the defendant's innocence, the prosecution moved that the charges be dropped.

   _____

   _____

   _____

5. The mayor's *malversation* came as a shock to the citizens. He had promised to clean up the corruption at City Hall, but in the end he too accepted a bribe.

_____

_____

_____

6. The *obverse* of a coin is called "heads." The reverse is called "tails."

_____

_____

_____

7. The best views can be seen from the *vertex* of a mountain. If you stand there, you can see for miles and miles.

_____

_____

_____

8. Staring at the *vertiginous* action of ceiling fans, pinwheels, and tops can sometimes hypnotize you.

_____

_____

_____

9. People who suffer from *vertigo* may not want to ride a merry-go-round, fly with a stunt pilot, or do cartwheels.

_____

_____

_____

10. Debris whirled about the *vortex* of the tornado as it snaked across the open field.

_____

_____

_____

Applying Meaning

Read each sentence or short passage below. Write "correct" on the answer line if the vocabulary word has been used correctly. Write "incorrect" on the answer line if the vocabulary word has been used incorrectly.

1. With quick thinking and even faster reflexes, the cyclist was able to *avert* a collision with the pedestrian.

2. The geometry teacher asked students to draw a horizontal and a *vertigo* line on the graph.

3. Accused of *malversation*, President Nixon resigned rather than face certain impeachment.

4. It was *obverse* that Tracy was frightened. His hands trembled, his knees shook, and his eyes were as large as saucers.

5. After reaching the *vertex*, the climbers were too exhausted to continue to the top of the mountain.

1. _____

2. _____

3. _____

4. _____

5. _____

For each word used incorrectly, write a sentence using the word properly.

_____

_____

_____

_____

_____

_____

_____

_____

_____

_____

_____

Decide which word in parentheses best completes the sentence. Then write the sentence, adding the missing word.

6. Because of Ashok's _____ to sweet foods, he celebrates his birthday with a casserole instead of a cake. (aversion; inadvertence)

_____

_____

_____

7. Watching the _____ motion of the hamsters' wheel, the cat did not notice that his tail was under the rocking chair. (obverse; vertiginous)

_____

_____

_____

8. Before Columbus's voyage many believed the Earth was flat, but they lacked the _____ evidence necessary to convince the skeptics. (inadvertent; incontrovertible)

_____

_____

_____

9. Micah was so uncomfortable amidst the objects in the antique shop that he _____ knocked a vase down. (inadvertently; aversively)

_____

_____

_____

10. Too late, Alexis grabbed for her gold chain as it slipped from her neck and was swallowed by a _____ of water in the drain. (vertex; vortex)

_____

_____

_____

	Bonus Word
●	**maelstrom**
	Maelstrom, which means "a large, violent whirlpool," is used metaphorically to mean "a turbulent situation." A legend claims that two magic millstones aboard a ship sailing the Norwegian Sea ground out so much salt that the ship foundered. The millstones continued to grind away underwater, creating a huge whirlpool.
	Write a Report: Use a dictionary and other resources to research the words below. In a short report, explain the origin of each word and its present definition.
	babel cologne donnybrook tarantula vaudeville

Name _____

How well do you remember the words you studied in Lessons 19 through 21? Take the following test covering the words from the last three lessons.

Part 1 Choose the Correct Meaning

Each question below includes a word in capital letters, followed by four words or phrases. Choose the word or phrase that is <u>closest</u> in meaning to the word in capital letters. Write the letter for your answer on the line provided.

Sample

| **S.** FINISH | (A) enjoy | (B) complete | **S.** ___**B**___ |
| | (C) destroy | (D) enlarge | |

| **1.** VORTEX | (A) summit | (B) whirlpool | **1.** _____ |
| | (C) diameter | (D) geometric shape | |

| **2.** SHIBBOLETH | (A) leg bone | (B) celebration | **2.** _____ |
| | (C) catchword | (D) coin | |

| **3.** AD INFINITUM | (A) endlessly | (B) timely | **3.** _____ |
| | (C) temporarily | (D) shortly | |

| **4.** AVERSION | (A) enthusiasm | (B) frustration | **4.** _____ |
| | (C) sympathy | (D) dislike | |

| **5.** DIDACTIC | (A) autocratic | (B) complicated | **5.** _____ |
| | (C) clever | (D) instructive | |

| **6.** INCONTROVERTIBLE | (A) questionable | (B) indisputable | **6.** _____ |
| | (C) unnoticeable | (D) contradictory | |

| **7.** JUGGERNAUT | (A) overpowering force | (B) trickery | **7.** _____ |
| | (C) part of the throat | (D) sailor | |

| **8.** CAUSE CÉLÈBRE | (A) disaster | (B) warning | **8.** _____ |
| | (C) reason to celebrate | (D) controversial issue | |

| **9.** VERTIGINOUS | (A) upright | (B) adjacent | **9.** _____ |
| | (C) revolving | (D) not moving | |

Go on to next page. ➤

10. INCISE (A) provoke (B) engrave 10. _____
(C) surround (D) erase

11. VERTEX (A) bottom (B) top 11. _____
(C) center (D) interior

12. CHUTZPAH (A) nerve (B) cowardice 12. _____
(C) anxiety (D) attentiveness

**13. PERSONA
    NON GRATA** (A) ungrateful (B) private 13. _____
(C) unwelcome (D) unknown

14. INADVERTENT (A) deliberate (B) inappropriate 14. _____
(C) foolish (D) accidental

15. SOLACE (A) advice (B) discouragement 15. _____
(C) comfort (D) apology

Part 2 Matching Words and Meanings

Match the definition in Column B with the word in Column A.
Write the letter of the correct definition on the answer line.

Column A	**Column B**	
16. avert	a. wealthy, important person	16. _____
17. nabob	b. dizziness	17. _____
18. malversation	c. turn away; prevent	18. _____
19. imbroglio	d. flexible	19. _____
20. quid pro quo	e. instruct; enlighten	20. _____
21. asymmetrical	f. misconduct in public office	21. _____
22. supple	g. complicated situation	22. _____
23. spare	h. uneven	23. _____
24. vertigo	i. not excessive	24. _____
25. edify	j. equal exchange	25. _____

Name _____

The Old Farmer's Almanac

Are you curious about the future, **agog** about the possibility of record winter snowfalls, **entranced** by world-record holders, or thoughtful about
what happened on a certain day one hundred years ago? *The Old Farmer's
Almanac* may be exactly the reading material you have been looking for.
5   The oldest continuing periodical in the United States, it was begun in
1792 by Robert B. Thomas of Massachusetts. Since its inception, it has fascinated people with its homespun **mélange** of fact, fun, and folklore.

Almanacs in general are among the earliest known published works. A
surviving Egyptian manuscript, written during the reign (1304–1237 B.C.)
10   of Ramses II, **enumerates** religious festivals, designates lucky and unlucky
days in black and red, and predicts the fortunes of children according to
their birthday. Much later, Christopher Columbus and other navigators
used a volume prepared by a contemporary German mathematician and
astronomer, Johann Müller, to plan their voyages.

15   As the editor of *The Old Farmer's Almanac* for fifty-four years, Thomas established the format and tone of the annual publication—busy pages
bulging with facts and **palaver**, offering knowledge, entertainment, and
instruction. A bit larger and longer than the early editions, the modern
almanacs have changed only a **scintilla**; Thomas's byline, the yellow cover,
20   and even the hole punched through the upper left corner (for convenient hanging) still **prevail**.

Although Thomas may have intended the book as winter fare for farmers
confined in front of their roaring fires, there is something for everyone
in *The Old Farmer's Almanac*. Past issues have offered such features as the
25   history of badminton, a list of unsung heroes, facts and fiction about pigs,
and advice about how to become a world-record holder. In the course of
two centuries, readers have been able to **glean** an incredible variety of
practical advice: cooking with flowers, the best time for planting late
radishes and lettuce, combating a cold with a chest-and-throat plaster
30   made of butter and onions, and banishing fire ants.

For its loyal readers, *The Old Farmer's Almanac* has an aura of **infallibility**
that extends even to the detailed weather forecasts for each region of the
country. Although these are made without reference to the thickness of
squirrels' tails or the color of wooly caterpillars' fur, the editors **allegedly**
35   claim no more than eighty percent accuracy. They don't take their pre-
dictions too seriously, perhaps agreeing with French essayist Michel
Eyquem de Montaigne's suggestion, "Let us give Nature a chance: she
knows her business better than we do." When you are planning your year
and conducting the business of your life, try *The Old Farmer's Almanac;*
40   even if it doesn't reign supreme in your home, at least you will be amused.

Words

agog	مشتاق وحیری بودن
allege	دلیل آوردن، ادّعا کردن، متّهم کردن
entrance	مسّت کابودن
enumerate	برشمردن
glean	خوشه چینی کردن، ذرّه ذرّه جمع آوری کردن
infallible	مصون از اشتباه، خطا ناپذیر
mélange	ترکیب، مخلوط
palaver	گفتگوی مفصّل، وراجی
prevail	چربیدن، غالب شدن، دوام آوردن
scintilla	جرقه، اثر

Unlocking Meaning

Each word in this lesson's word list appears in dark type in the selection you just read. Think about how the vocabulary word is used in the selection, then write the letter for the best answer to each question.

1. Which word or words could best replace *agog* in line 1?
   (A) active   (B) in proper working order
   (C) being unequaled   ✓(D) eagerly excited

1. _____

2. Which word or words could best replace *entranced* in line 2?
   (A) altered   ✓(B) filled with wonder
   (C) overcome by uncertainty   (D) criticized

2. _____

3. A *mélange* (line 7) can best be described as _____.
   (A) one who has little talent   (B) material comfort
   ✓(C) a mixture   (D) peaceful relationships

3. _____

4. Which word or words could best replace *enumerates* in line 10?
   ✓(A) lists   (B) makes more powerful
   (C) denounces   (D) becomes accountable

4. _____

5. *Palaver* (line 17) can best be explained as _____.
   (A) one that precedes another   ✓(B) chatter
   (C) an extravagant act   (D) an object of aversion

5. _____

6. Which word or words could best replace *scintilla* in line 19?
   (A) contradiction   (B) brief statement
   (C) earlier period   ✓(D) trace

6. _____

7. Which words could best replace *prevail* in line 21?
   (A) urgently request   (B) express approval
   ✓(C) continue in use   (D) come near or close

7. _____

8. Which word or words could best replace *glean* in line 27?
   ✓(A) collect bit by bit   (B) misinterpret
   (C) dispute   (D) attack and capture

8. _____

9. *Infallibility* (line 31) can best be explained as _____.
   (A) a typical product or result   (B) a fiery intensity of feeling
   (C) a far-reaching policy   ✓(D) the quality of being free from errors

9. _____

10. Which word or words could best replace *allegedly* in line 34?
    (A) in a bad manner   (B) proudly
    ✓(C) supposedly   (D) hurriedly

10. _____

Applying Meaning

Decide which word in parentheses best completes the sentence. Then write the sentence, adding the missing word.

1. Since several of his guests were vegetarians, Vijay prepared a large bowl of pasta and a _____ of grilled vegetables in a balsamic vinegar glaze. (mélange; palaver)

_____

_____

_____

2. DeVona happily _____ all the things she liked about her job. (enumerated; prevailed)

_____

_____

_____

3. All the children in the audience loved the new animated film; even the three- and four-year-olds sat _____, their eyes glued to the screen. (entranced; infallible)

_____

_____

_____

4. Even though their team was behind by a touchdown late in the fourth quarter, the fans were hopeful that their team would _____. (allege; prevail)

_____

_____

_____

5. The teenagers were _____ at the prospect of having a popular rock musician living next door. (agog; infallible)

_____

_____

_____

6. The burglary was _____ committed during the parade, but detectives could not figure out how the culprit entered the building without being seen. (allegedly; infallibly)

_____

_____

_____

7. It was not surprising that Pam's wallet was stolen from her purse; she showed not a _____ of sense when she left it on the counter while she tried on some shoes. (mélange; scintilla)

_____

_____

_____

8. When the archaeologist returned from Guatemala, she assembled an exhibit of the _____ from her most recent dig. (gleanings; palaver)

_____

_____

_____

9. We thought Professor Hanks was _____ until he confessed he couldn't name the author of *The Good Earth*. (entranced; infallible)

_____

_____

_____

10. Uncertain of exactly how to get the meeting under way, Mr. Hsu was hesitant to interrupt the audience's _____. (palaver; scintilla)

_____

_____

_____

Mastering Meaning

Choose a magazine intended for readers your age. Write a critical review of the magazine, commenting on design, editorial philosophy, the quality of the writing, and any other aspect of the publication that interests you. Use some of the words you have studied in this lesson.

Name _____

Although many people thrive on the bustle and commotion of everyday life, everyone needs occasional calm interludes to restore energy. A quiet evening at home or an hour sitting under a tree can do wonders. Times of tranquility can renew physical, mental, and emotional vigor. The ten words in this lesson will help you describe peaceful people, places, and times.

Unlocking Meaning

Read the sentences or short passages below. Write the letter for the correct definition of the italicized vocabulary word.

The Stamoses decided to hold their argument in *abeyance* until they finished dinner; they knew from experience that heated debate is not good for digestion.

1. (A) a source of risk
   (B) temporary suspension
   (C) high priority
   (D) deterioration

We enjoyed meeting Gus yesterday. On first impression, he seemed to be *affable*, outgoing, and warm.

2. (A) easy and pleasant to speak to
   (B) obnoxious
   (C) self-indulgent
   (D) angry

The *bucolic* settings of John Constable's paintings seem to lure viewers into the inviting landscape to wander a winding lane or perch on a fence.

3. (A) diseased
   (B) deteriorating
   (C) boldly resisting
   (D) rural

In spite of his fame, tenor Enrico Caruso never became *complacent*. He continued to study opera and voice throughout his brilliant career.

4. (A) authoritative
   (B) self-satisfied and unconcerned
   (C) undignified
   (D) frail in constitution

Words
abeyance
affable
bucolic
complacent
concord
halcyon
imperturbable
inert
pacific
pliable

1. _____

2. _____

3. _____

4. _____

Hugh and Beth discovered during the course of the evening that they were in *concord* on just about every topic that arose, from the poetry of Edgar Allan Poe to the music of Harry Connick Jr.

5. (A) social equality

5. _____

(B) state of depression

(C) agreement

(D) reckless mischief

For the exhausted boaters, the *halcyon* weather provided a brief respite from danger and worry.

6. (A) calm and peaceful

6. _____

(B) stormy

(C) affectionate

(D) powerful

Usually *imperturbable*, Silas was quite irritable and moody during final exams.

7. _____

7. (A) diabolic

(B) harsh sounding

(C) gloomy

(D) unshakably calm and collected

After the oil spill, the beach was littered with hundreds of *inert* sea otters.

8. (A) noisy

8. _____

(B) reluctant

(C) sluggish or unable to move

(D) scatterbrained

My mother has a *pacific* approach to fights in our family. Instead of taking sides or punishing us, she tries to help us settle our differences.

9. (A) easily brought to tears

9. _____

(B) tending to lessen conflict

(C) ridiculous

(D) easily angered

Terry wished that he could be more *pliable*. Each time he and his family moved to a new city, he underwent months of unhappiness and stress until he felt at home.

10. (A) adaptable to change

10. _____

(B) amusingly odd

(C) pleasing in appearance

(D) intense

Applying Meaning

Read each sentence below. Write "correct" on the answer line if the vocabulary word has been used correctly. Write "incorrect" on the answer line if the vocabulary word has been used incorrectly.

1. Many grandparents like to recall the *halcyon* days of their youth, when movies cost a nickel and people never had to lock their doors.

2. Traders and merchants who crossed the great expanses of desert in the Middle East used camels as their *abeyance*.

3. A noble in the court of Richard III was sentenced to life imprisonment in the Tower of London for *bucolic* crimes.

4. The *pliable* young maple tree survived the violent thunderstorm, while the ancient oak tree was completely uprooted.

5. The story of the *imperturbable* Dutch boy who placed his finger in a leaking dike to save a town from a flood is actually an American invention.

1. _____

2. _____

3. _____

4. _____

5. _____

For each word used incorrectly, write a sentence using the word properly.

_____

_____

_____

_____

_____

_____

_____

_____

_____

Write each sentence below. In the space write a form of the word in parentheses. The form of the word in parentheses may be correct.

6. As the _____ notes of the overture sounded, the audience quieted in anticipation. (concord)

_____

_____

_____

7. Ms. Feldman's patience, kindness, and _____ made her the most sought-after school counselor. (affable)

_____

_____

_____

8. The candidate criticized the mayor and the town council for their _____ and indecisiveness. (inert)

_____

_____

_____

9. Mr. Louis's _____ nature has made him the perfect mediator in disputes between management and employees. (pacific)

_____

_____

_____

10. Melva's _____ was shaken when she did poorly on a test she had expected to pass easily. (complacent)

_____

_____

_____

Our Living Language

One of the words in this lesson, *halcyon*, comes from a Greek legend. Alcyone, daughter of the wind god Aeolus, drowned herself in the sea. Punishing the suicide, the angry gods turned both Alcyone and her husband into birds, called *halcyons*. Aeolus took pity on the couple and decreed that during the birds' nesting season, the fourteen days before and after the shortest day of the year, the sea would always be perfectly calm so that the birds' eggs could lie undisturbed on the water. These days once had an actual place on the calendar, but eventually the phrase "halcyon days" came to mean any time of peace and serenity.

Use the Library: Do some research on one of the birds listed below. In a brief report, explain the history or legend that surrounds the creature and what other meanings the word has today.

| albatross | phoenix | dodo | roc | raven |

Copyright © Glencoe/McGraw-Hill, a division of The McGraw-Hill Companies, Inc.

106 Vocabulary of Peace and Tranquility

The Roots -nomen- , -nomin-, *and* -onym-

Name _____

The roots *-nomen-* and *-nomin-*, from the Latin word *nomen*, mean "name." The root *-onym-*, from the Greek word *onyma*, also means "name." Many words you already know contain one of these roots. For example, if you *nominate* someone to a school office, you propose that person by name as a candidate. In this lesson you will learn other words that are derived from these roots.

Root	Meaning	English Word
-nomen-	name	misnomer
-nomin-		denomination
-onym-		acronym

Unlocking Meaning

Write the vocabulary word that fits each clue below. Then say the word and write a short definition. Compare your definition and pronunciation with those given on the flash card.

1. This noun is often used to "name" religious groups or kinds and values of currency.

   _____

   _____

   _____

2. This noun has the prefix *-a-*, meaning "without." While some people seek stardom and want to be famous, others prefer this.

   _____

   _____

   _____

3. This noun starts with the Greek word part *-acro-*, meaning "beginning." "ROM" and "NASA" are two examples of this.

   _____

   _____

   _____

Words

- **acronym**
- **anonymity**
- **denomination**
- **homonym**
- **ignominy**
- **metonymy**
- **misnomer**
- **nomenclature**
- **nominal**
- **pseudonym**

4. This word is usually an adjective. Someone who has a job title without the actual responsibility that goes with it probably has this kind of role.

_____

_____

_____

5. This noun begins with a form of the Greek word part *-meta-*. You are using this figure of speech if you refer to the king as "the crown."

_____

_____

_____

6. This noun combines the Greek word *homos,* meaning "same," with a "name" root. It refers to words like *sea* and *see.*

_____

_____

_____

7. This noun has a prefix meaning "false." A famous person who wants to disguise his or her identity might use this.

_____

_____

_____

8. This noun contains part of the Latin word *calare,* meaning "to call." A science textbook defines this in the glossary.

_____

_____

_____

9. This noun begins with the same prefix as *misunderstand.* Naming a pure-white cat "Stripes" is an example of this.

_____

_____

_____

10. This noun begins with a variation of the prefix *-in-,* meaning "not." Someone who experiences this may not want to show his or her face.

_____

_____

_____

Applying Meaning

Decide which word in parentheses best completes the sentence. Then write the sentence, adding the missing word.

1. When filling out a census form, you are sometimes asked to indicate your religious _____. (acronym; denomination)

    _____

    _____

    _____

2. The _____ of his conviction for armed robbery would haunt his family for years. (anonymity; ignominy)

    _____

    _____

    _____

3. In the mistaken belief that he had reached the East Indies, Christopher Columbus gave the residents he found in the new land the _____ "Indians." (misnomer; homonym)

    _____

    _____

    _____

4. "Richard Bachman" was the _____ used by author Stephen King when he wanted to experiment with different types of fiction that he wasn't sure his readers would accept. (acronym; pseudonym)

    _____

    _____

    _____

5. In the _____ of architecture, Ionic columns are slender and finely fluted while Doric columns are heavy and thickly fluted. (misnomer; nomenclature)

    _____

    _____

    _____

Each question below contains a vocabulary word from this lesson. Answer each question "yes" or "no" in the space provided.

6. Are *acronyms* shorter and easier to remember than the expressions they represent?

6. _____

7. When someone is nominated for a position, does he or she then become the *nominal*?

7. _____

8. Would someone who wants to maintain his or her *anonymity* be likely to wear a nametag at a social gathering?

8. _____

9. Was Edward Bulwer-Lytton using *metonymy* when he said, "The pen is mightier than the sword"?

9. _____

10. Do religious services often conclude with the choir singing a *homonym*?

10. _____

For each question you answered "no," write a sentence using the vocabulary word correctly.

_____

_____

_____

_____

_____

_____

_____

_____

_____

_____

Our Living Language

Acronyms are formed by combining the initial letters or parts of a series of words to create a new word. For example, the familiar word *radar* was formed from the words <u>ra</u>dio <u>d</u>etecting <u>a</u>nd <u>r</u>anging. Here are some other examples you may recognize:

NATO   <u>N</u>orth <u>A</u>tlantic <u>T</u>reaty <u>O</u>rganization

scuba   <u>s</u>elf <u>c</u>ontained <u>u</u>nderwater <u>b</u>reathing <u>a</u>pparatus

ZIP (code) <u>Z</u>oning <u>I</u>mprovement <u>P</u>lan

Cooperative Learning: Technology has been the source of many new acronyms, like *CD-ROM* and *modem*. Work with a group of your classmates to create a dictionary of computer-related acronyms. List the terms in alphabetical order and spell out the source of each acronym, following the model above.

Name _____

How well do you remember the words you studied in Lessons 22 through 24? Take the following test covering the words from the last three lessons.

Part 1 Antonyms

Each question below includes a word in capital letters, followed by four words or phrases. Choose the word or phrase that is most nearly <u>opposite</u> in meaning to the word in capital letters. Consider all choices before deciding on your answer. Write the letter for your answer on the line provided.

Sample

S. HIGH	(A) cold	(B) simple	**S.** ____**C**____
	(C) low	(D) foolish	

1. ABEYANCE   (A) suspension   (B) conformity   **1.** _____
                         (C) obedience   (D) vigorous activity

2. PLIABLE   (A) rigid   (B) abundant   **2.** _____
                         (C) aggravated   (D) adaptable

3. ENTRANCE   (A) diminish   (B) delight   **3.** _____
                         (C) bore   (D) persuade

4. AFFABLE   (A) agreeable   (B) humorous   **4.** _____
                         (C) emotional   (D) easily irritated

5. ANONYMITY   (A) disguise   (B) recognition   **5.** _____
                         (C) investment   (D) nuisance

6. PACIFIC   (A) turbulent   (B) tranquil   **6.** _____
                         (C) strenuous   (D) refreshing

7. BUCOLIC   (A) rustic   (B) sickly   **7.** _____
                         (C) urban   (D) monotonous

8. IGNOMINY   (A) honor   (B) intelligence   **8.** _____
                         (C) reputation   (D) humiliation

9. INERT   (A) lifeless   (B) incompetent   **9.** _____
                         (C) active   (D) suitable

10. INFALLIBLE   (A) interior   (B) unreliable   **10.** _____
                         (C) shameful   (D) trustworthy

Go on to next page. ➤

Part 2 Matching Words and Meanings

Match the definition in Column B with the word in Column A.
Write the letter of the correct definition on the answer line.

Column A	Column B	
11. concord	a. incorrect name	**11.** _____
12. acronym	b. continue to be used	**12.** _____
13. misnomer	c. chatter	**13.** _____
14. halcyon	d. name or designation	**14.** _____
15. scintilla	e. agreement	**15.** _____
16. denomination	f. mixture	**16.** _____
17. nomenclature	g. calm and peaceful	**17.** _____
18. palaver	h. system of names	**18.** _____
19. mélange	i. tiny amount	**19.** _____
20. glean	j. a word made up of initials	**20.** _____
21. enumerate	k. excited	**21.** _____
22. pseudonym	l. gather	**22.** _____
23. agog	m. self-satisfied	**23.** _____
24. prevail	n. fictitious name	**24.** _____
25. complacent	o. list	**25.** _____

Name _____

Zapped by a Cat

Have you ever been zapped by a cat? If so, you're not the first person to stroll across a nylon carpet in a warm, dry room to pick up your favorite **feline,** only to be greeted by a crackling **fusillade** of stinging sparks.

5   Nearly everyone knows the discomfort of a static electric shock. Because we tend to think of electricity as something that flows through wires, getting zapped by a cat or a doorknob comes as quite a surprise. Some days you can become downright **paranoid** when all the objects around you seem to want to unleash a tiny bolt of lightning in your direction. But, in fact, your cat and the objects in the room have no such **vendetta** against

10 you; it's only nature at work.

To understand static electricity, you need to recall the familiar model of an atom, with its nucleus of positively charged protons and their **antipodes**, the negatively charged electrons, whirling about them. Some substances, such as nylon, have only a loose hold on those negatively

15 charged electrons, so as you casually glide across a nylon carpet your feet pick up some of them. By the time you reach the cat, your body has acquired a negative electrical charge.

Like the nylon in the carpet, a cat's fur also tends to lose its negatively charged electrons in warm, dry air or through the gentle stroking

20 provided by an admiring cat lover. By losing its negatively charged electrons, the cat's fur acquires a positive charge. Because the positive charges in each strand of fur repel each other, you may note a change in the cat's **coiffure** — its hair may stand straight up. When your negatively charged hand approaches the positively charged cat, they neu-

25 tralize each other with a zap. While an observer might find such a **salvo** of sparks quite **risible,** the victim of such a shock usually finds it anything but amusing.

The effects of static electricity can be demonstrated in another way. When a **glabrous** item, such as an inflated balloon, is rubbed on a wool or nylon

30 sweater, its smooth surface picks up an excess of negatively charged electrons. Then, when it is held against a plaster wall, the balloon attracts the positive charges in the wall, causing it to "stick." Only after the positive and negative charges have been exchanged and neutralized will the balloon fall to the floor.

35 In spite of the drama and discomfort of static electricity, you never hear of anyone being killed or **debilitated** by it. Electrical shocks must have billions of electrons to injure or kill. In nature, only lightning carries this dangerous level of electric charge.

Copyright © Glencoe/McGraw-Hill, a division of The McGraw-Hill Companies, Inc.

Words

antipode
coiffure
debilitate
feline
fusillade
glabrous
paranoid
risible
salvo
vendetta

Each word in this lesson's word list appears in dark type in the selection you just read. Think about how the vocabulary word is used in the selection, then write the letter for the best answer to each question.

1. In line 3, the word *feline* means ___.

   (A) carpet   (B) an electrical device

   (C) laundry   ✓(D) a member of the cat family

1. _____

2. Which word or words could best replace *fusillade* in line 3?

   (A) fancy clothing   (B) musical sound

   (C) compliment   ✓(D) rapid outburst

2. _____

3. In line 7, the word *paranoid* means ___.

  ✓(A) extremely fearful   (B) carefree

   (C) sleepy   (D) devout

3. _____

4. Which word or words could best replace *vendetta* in line 9?

   (A) kind appearance   (B) physical deformity

   (C) bright color   ✓(D) bitter feud

4. _____

5. Which word or words could best replace *antipodes* in line 13?

   (A) dangers   (B) unusual appearances

   (C) clever imitations   ✓(D) opposites

5. _____

6. Which word or words could best replace *coiffure* in line 23?

   (A) eating habits   ✓(B) hairstyle

   (C) attitude toward work   (D) location

6. _____

7. A *salvo* (line 25) is a(n) _____.

  ✓(A) sudden burst; attack   (B) type of medicine

   (C) encouraging remark   (D) blessing

7. _____

8. Which word could best replace *risible* in line 26?

   (A) sensible   (B) political

  ✓(C) laughable   (D) rewarding

8. _____

9. Which word could best replace *glabrous* in line 29?

  ✓(A) smooth; fur-free   (B) loud

   (C) heavy   (D) handsome

9. _____

10. In line 36, the word *debilitated* means _____.

   (A) enlightened   (B) deceived

  ✓(C) weakened   (D) excused

10. _____

Applying Meaning

Read each sentence below. Write "correct" on the answer line if the vocabulary word has been used correctly. Write "incorrect" on the answer line if the vocabulary word has been used incorrectly.

1. Maria's *coiffure* was very elegant, incorporating hundreds of curls and rhinestone-studded combs.

    1. *Correct*

2. We hired an exterminator to rid our basement of an infestation of *antipodes*.

    2. *Incorrect*

3. Since cars and trucks were barely *risible* [*visible*] in the thick fog, there were several accidents on the freeway that day.

    3. *Incorrect*

4. Frogs and many other amphibians have *glabrous* skin.

    4. *Correct*

5. Ever since he lost his leg to the white whale, Captain Ahab had carried on a personal *vendetta* against the creature.

    5. *Correct*

6. The mother soothed the frightened child with reassuring, gentle *salvos*.

    6. *Incorrect*

For each word used incorrectly, write a sentence using the word properly.

_____

_____

_____

_____

_____

_____

_____

_____

_____

_____

_____

_____

_____

_____

_____

_____

Each question below contains at least one vocabulary word from this lesson. Answer each question "yes" or "no" in the space provided.

7. Is a handicapped cat a *debilitated feline?*

8. If everyone in class had a *vendetta* against you, would you feel a little *paranoid?*

Antipodes of its body.

9. Are the wings of an airplane attached to the *fusillade?*

10. Would you ask your hairdresser to give you a *risible coiffure* before your first job interview?

For each question you answered "no," write a sentence using the vocabulary word(s) correctly.

7. Yes

8. Yes

9. No

10. No

_____

_____

_____

_____

_____

_____

_____

_____

_____

_____

_____

_____

Mastering Meaning

Write a short narrative about an embarrassing or painful event — real or imaginary — involving electricity. Use some of the words you studied in this lesson.

Name _____

"Status" refers to the relative position of an individual or a group within a larger group. Although many people are constantly striving to improve their status, the Roman historian Sallust warned that ". . . in the highest position there is the least freedom of action." The ten words in this lesson will help you evaluate existing circumstances and people's standing given those circumstances.

Words
austere
bourgeois
caste
dilettante
éclat
indigent
munificent
plebeian
provincial
sycophant

Unlocking Meaning

Read the sentences or short passages below. Write the letter for the correct definition of the italicized vocabulary word.

The *austere* clothing worn by members of the religious order reflected their humble and modest lifestyle.

1.　(A) untidy
　　(B) outrageous
　　(C) cluttered
　✓(D) simple and plain

Their next-door neighbor accused the Millers of having *bourgeois* values, citing their trendy new cars and lavish parties as proof.

2.　(A) ultra-religious
　✓(B) preoccupied with middle-class social and material interests
　　(C) concerned with helping the less fortunate
　　(D) independent

In India, people born in a particular *caste* are restricted in their choice of occupation and their association with people of other castes. In other countries wealth or other factors can have the same effect.

1. _____

3.✓(A) social class based on wealth, inherited rank, or profession
　　(B) the practice of exaggerating one's own importance
　　(C) the act of concealing something in a hiding place
　　(D) one of several components

2. _____

The millionaire's son, with no need to work for a living, has become a *dilettante*. He spends his time playing at his computer, experimenting in the kitchen, or fixing up antique automobiles.

3. _____

4.　(A) a person regarded as irrational
　　(B) a part-time employee
　✓(C) a dabbler in a field of knowledge
　　(D) a socialite

4. _____

As a pianist, Jason showed *éclat* at a young age. His teacher claimed she had never seen anyone learn so quickly.

5. (A) lethargy

   ✓(B) brilliance

   (C) long fingers

   (D) immaturity

5. _____

Indigent farm workers camped outside the orchard, hoping for a chance to pick late peaches or early apples to earn enough money to buy food and fuel.

6. ✓(A) poor or needy

   (B) regarded as sacred

   (C) immune from criticism

   (D) noisy

6. _____

Some wealthy families, such as the Rockefellers and the Carnegies, have made *munificent* contributions to create museums and libraries for public use.

7. (A) merciless

   (B) weakened by neglect

   (C) meager

   ✓(D) generous

7. _____

Grandmother believes that people who chew gum loudly and men who wear hats indoors have *plebeian* manners.

8. (A) full of health

   ✓(B) crude and unrefined

   (C) noisy or lively

   (D) kept within limits

8. _____

Having lived in a small town all their lives, the Thralls had *provincial* taste in food. They had never eaten lobster or scallops, and they had never heard of zabaglione, the delicious custard sauce served with fruit.

9. (A) slow in physical development

   (B) adventuresome

   ✓(C) narrow and unsophisticated

   (D) characteristic of urban life

9. _____

When she heard his name was Paul Mellin, Daphne gushed a welcome to the new club member, complimenting him on his good sense in joining. What this *sycophant* did not realize was that there is a large difference in social status between the wealthy Mellon and the impoverished Mellin families.

10. (A) one who is mentally unstable

   ✓(B) one who seeks favor by flattering influential people

   (C) one who is playfully mischievous

   (D) a member of a tumultuous crowd

10. _____

Applying Meaning

Follow the directions below to write a sentence using a vocabulary word.

1. Use any form of the word *austere* to describe the living conditions or lifestyle of an individual or group.

   Religons force their followers to austere living to reach a without austere living in another world.

2. Tell about a unique gift. Use any form of the word *munificent*.

   That Musical box was munificent, but I love its color and its nice music.

3. Explain a political or social system. Use the word *caste*.

   Any caste has its own rules and its members must follow them strictly.

4. Use any form of the word *sycophant* to describe the behavior of one or more people.

   Don't be a sycophant

5. Describe the attitude an accomplished professional might have toward an amateur or someone less committed to perfection. Use any form of the word *dilettante*.

   _____

   _____

   _____

Decide which word in parentheses best completes the sentence. Then write the sentence, adding the missing word.

6. Monroe's ____ manners became quite evident at the wedding reception when he tucked his napkin under his chin. (munificent; provincial)

   _____

   _____

   _____

lining

voile

7. Immigrants in turn-of-the-century America were called "greenhorns"; thought to be _____, they were simply inexperienced in the ways of this country. (munificent; plebeian)

_____

_____

_____

8. For _____ homeowners in fourteenth-century Italy, a tower was the ultimate status symbol. (indigent; bourgeois)

_____

_____

_____

9. The bill proposed aid for the _____ people who roamed the streets by day and slept in cardboard boxes at night. (indigent; sycophantic)

_____

_____

_____

10. Although they modestly claimed to have no special gift for music, the twins demonstrated _____ each time they performed. (caste; éclat)

_____

_____

_____

Cultural Literacy Note

Bourgeois and *éclat* are just two of many words directly borrowed from French. The conquest of England by the Normans from northwestern France in 1066 brought great changes to English culture and to the English language. By 1100 Norman French had become the language of the dominant classes in England, and Old English was relegated to the speech of peasants and workers. By the thirteenth century, the Normans began to consider England their home and gradually started to use English rather than French. By that time, however, they had introduced thousands of French words and expressions into the English vocabulary.

Use a Dictionary: Look up the following words and write a definition for each. Then write an original sentence using each word correctly.

adroit	avant garde	chateau	
forte	gauche	nonchalant	rendezvous

The Roots -pend- and -pens-

Name _____

The root *-pend-* comes from the Latin word *pendere,* meaning "to weigh," "to hang," or "to pay." The root *-pens-* comes from the Latin word *pensare,* meaning "to weigh" or "to ponder." Both of these roots have contributed many words to the English language. For example, if you *depend* on people, you rely, or "hang," on them for support or maintenance. The ten words in this lesson each contain one of these roots.

Root	Meaning	English Word
-pend-	to hang, to weigh, to pay	compendium
-pens-	to weigh, to ponder	pensive

Words

appendage

compendium

equipoise

expendable

penchant

pensive

perpend

prepense

propensity

stipend

Unlocking Meaning

A vocabulary word appears in italics in each sentence or short passage below. Find the root in each vocabulary word and choose the letter for the correct definition. Write the letter for your answer on the line provided.

Ms. Ghash recommends adding an *appendage,* such as a graph or chart, to our reports, in order to illustrate our facts and statistics.

1. (A) something attached to a larger entity
   (B) judicial procedure
   (C) thing that serves as an obstacle
   (D) fundamental principle

Angel is preparing a *compendium* of accessible CD-ROM resources.

2. (A) a religious shrine
   (B) an abrupt transition
   (C) a list or collection of items
   (D) an intense argument for

My parents say they will consider me mature when I take responsibility for my actions and achieve emotional *equipoise.*

3. (A) politeness
   (B) equilibrium or balance
   (C) support
   (D) status

In an effort to make room for his car, my father cleaned out the garage and discarded all the things he considered *expendable.*

4. (A) in good condition
   (B) useful
   (C) pleasing to the eye
   (D) not strictly necessary

1. _____

2. _____

3. _____

4. _____

It's obvious that the cat has a *penchant* for sunny windows and tuna tidbits. He always leaps from the kitchen windowsill and runs to his dish when he smells fish.

5. (A) explanation   5. _____
   (B) definite liking
   (C) dislike
   (D) lack of appreciation

In a *pensive* mood, Rowena spent the day listening to music, looking through photo albums, and wishing she were back in Paris.

6. (A) suggestive of doing good deeds   6. _____
   (B) surpassing all others
   (C) dreamily thoughtful
   (D) more useful

To come to a fair decision, a jury needs to *perpend* all of the evidence and testimony that has been presented.

7. (A) reflect on carefully   7. _____
   (B) squabble about
   (C) divide into parts
   (D) obstruct

Our legal system makes a distinction between murders committed spontaneously in the heat of passion and *prepense* murders committed as the result of a conscious plan.

8. (A) unsolved   8. _____
   (B) spectacular
   (C) trustworthy
   (D) decided in advance

Considering that several members of his family are artists, it is not surprising that Deryl has a *propensity* for graphic design and has decided to make it his career.

9. (A) lack of talent   9. _____
   (B) inclination or tendency
   (C) unusual name
   (D) dislike

The TV ratings company gives its test viewers a monthly *stipend* to cover the cost of using each television set in their homes.

10. (A) fixed payment   10. _____
    (B) advertisement
    (C) program
    (D) bargain

Applying Meaning

Read each sentence or short passage below. Write "correct" on the answer line if the vocabulary word has been used correctly. Write "incorrect" on the answer line if the vocabulary word has been used incorrectly.

1. At the used-book sale, my brother was able to purchase a *compendium* of Shakespeare's most famous tragedies at a bargain price.

2. Judith Martin, who calls herself "Miss Manners," has written many newspaper columns and books about *equipoise*.

3. As the tadpole grew, the children watched with great interest its vanishing *appendage*.

4. Lana was thrilled with the moonstone and silver *penchant* that her aunt and uncle gave her for graduation.

5. Because it was built on a large lot, the house was easily *expendable;* there was plenty of land for adding on more rooms.

1. _____

2. _____

3. _____

4. _____

5. _____

For each word used incorrectly, write a sentence using the word properly.

_____

_____

_____

_____

_____

_____

_____

_____

_____

_____

_____

_____

Follow the directions below to write a sentence using a vocabulary word.

6. Comment on a summer or after-school job that you have had and the wages you received. Use the word *stipend*.

_____

_____

_____

7. Describe a characteristic or habit that seems to run in a family. Use the word *propensity*.

_____   _____

_____

_____

8. Describe someone daydreaming. Use any form of the word *pensive*.

_____

_____

_____

9. Describe a misunderstanding between two people. Use any form of the word *prepense*.

_____

_____

_____

10. Tell about the actions of a contestant on a television game show. Use the word *perpend*.

_____

_____

_____

Test-Taking Strategies

An antonym test asks you to choose the word that is most nearly <u>opposite</u> in meaning to another word.

Sample

| **S.** CAUTIOUS | (A) hurtful | (B) wary | **S.** _____ **C** _____ |
| | (C) daring | (D) humiliated | |

Because this type of test asks you to distinguish between words with slightly different meanings, it is good to look at all the choices before answering. Also, be careful *not* to choose a synonym as your answer.
Practice: Choose the word that is most nearly <u>opposite</u> in meaning to the word in capital letters.

| **1.** PENNILESS | (A) needy | (B) mute | **1.** _____ |
| | (C) affluent | (D) fashionable | |

| **2.** SANITIZE | (A) pollute | (B) fulfill | **2.** _____ |
| | (C) embezzle | (D) propagate | |

| **3.** OBSTACLE | (A) function | (B) uproar | **3.** _____ |
| | (C) hurdle | (D) aid | |

Name _____

How well do you remember the words you studied in Lessons 25 through 27? Take the following test covering the words from the last three lessons.

Part 1 Choose the Correct Meaning

Each question below includes a word in capital letters, followed by four words or phrases. Choose the word or phrase that is <u>closest</u> in meaning to the word in capital letters. Write the letter for your answer on the line provided.

Sample

S. FINISH	(A) complete	(B) enjoy	**S.**	**A**
	(C) destroy	(D) enlarge		

1. PENSIVE   (A) critical   (B) dreamily thoughtful   **1.** _____

                    (C) cranky   (D) good-natured

2. INDIGENT   (A) furious   (B) self-reliant   **2.** _____

                    (C) poor   (D) wealthy

3. RISIBLE   (A) easily irritated   (B) laughable   **3.** _____

                    (C) slippery   (D) demanding

4. VENDETTA   (A) feud   (B) musical term   **4.** _____

                    (C) street merchant   (D) inspirational message

5. PROVINCIAL   (A) outgoing   (B) dignified   **5.** _____

                    (C) unsophisticated   (D) modern

6. EXPENDABLE   (A) nonessential   (B) important   **6.** _____

                    (C) elastic   (D) widespread

7. PENCHANT   (A) hatred   (B) liveliness   **7.** _____

                    (C) enclosure   (D) fondness

8. MUNIFICENT   (A) brilliant   (B) generous   **8.** _____

                    (C) selfish   (D) magnificent

9. SALVO   (A) ointment   (B) genius   **9.** _____

                    (C) reward   (D) sudden burst

Go on to next page. ➤

10. AUSTERE   (A) fortunate   (B) kindly   10. _____

                   (C) simple   (D) radical

11. PROPENSITY   (A) inclination   (B) superiority   11. _____

                   (C) hypothesis   (D) dislike

12. ÉCLAT   (A) pastry   (B) overshadowing   12. _____

                   (C) imitation   (D) brilliance

13. PLEBEIAN   (A) superior   (B) crude   13. _____

                   (C) talented   (D) realistic

14. PERPEND   (A) consent   (B) suggest   14. _____

                   (C) commit   (D) consider carefully

15. EQUIPOISE   (A) balance   (B) disproportion   15. _____

                   (C) gear   (D) fairness

Part 2 Matching Words and Meanings

Match the definition in Column B with the word in Column A.
Write the letter of the correct definition on the line provided.

Column A   **Column B**

16. feline   a. hairstyle   16. _____

17. coiffure   b. list   17. _____

18. bourgeois   c. arranged in advance   18. _____

19. stipend   d. dabbler in a field of knowledge   19. _____

20. compendium   e. cat   20. _____

21. dilettante   f. fixed payment   21. _____

22. sycophant   g. rigid class system   22. _____

23. prepense   h. smooth and hairless   23. _____

24. caste   i. self-seeking flatterer   24. _____

25. glabrous   j. having middle-class interests   25. _____

Name _____

Across and Down

Do you begin each day by folding a newspaper and escaping to a quiet workplace where every problem has a solution—if only you can figure it out? If so, you are among the millions of people who indulge in the most popular and widespread word game in the world—the crossword puzzle.

5   The first puzzle was a **whimsical** holiday gift of sorts. Arthur Wynne, a newspaper editor, was looking for a way to enliven the 1913 Christmas edition of the *New York World* Sunday magazine. He drew a diamond-shaped grid and fashioned a puzzle of thirty-two interlocking words that he called "Word Cross." Although it became a regular Sunday feature, the game did
10 not really take off until 1924, when Simon and Schuster published the first book devoted to the puzzles.

It wasn't long before solving crossword puzzles became a national **compulsion**. Sales of dictionaries and thesauri rose, and restaurants printed the black-and-white grids on the backs of their menus. **Exasperated** zoo
15 officials announced that they would no longer answer questions about gnus, emus, or any other animals with three-letter names. These early puzzles were relatively simple, consisting mainly of one-word solutions based on current events and general information. Over the years, crosswords became unimaginative and predictable.

20 It is **ironic** that the crossword puzzle revival was led by a major newspaper that had held out against the craze. In 1924 the *New York Times* had bemoaned the game's prevalence as "a primitive form of mental exercise" and predicted its swift demise. Obviously unsuccessful in **extirpating** crosswords, the *Times* finally **capitulated** and published its own puzzle in 1942.
25 Its Sunday and daily versions, introduced a few years later, soon established themselves as the standard of excellence.

The *New York Times* puzzle editors were instrumental in establishing many of the rules that continue to govern the creation of crosswords: the grid must be entirely interconnected; the briefer the clue, the better; and no
30 two-letter words are permitted. It is also considered bad form to have two **obscure** words intersect. Puzzle makers are expected to avoid "crosswordese"—**abstruse** words that, because of convenient vowel-consonant combinations, have been overused. Despite these rules, some crosswords are difficult enough to tempt the frustrated to abandon their personal
35 **ethics** temporarily, and turn to the solution page for some answers.

Aficionados regard crossword puzzles as much more than entertainment. Revolving around themes and filled with truncated words, puns, hidden meanings, proper names, and foreign terms, the puzzles build vocabulary, test spelling, and challenge general knowledge.

Words
abstruse
aficionado
capitulate
compulsion
ethics
exasperate
extirpate
ironic
obscure
whimsical

Unlocking Meaning

Each word in this lesson's word list appears in dark type in the selection you just read. Think about how the vocabulary word is used in the selection, then write the letter for the best answer to each question.

1. Which word could best replace *whimsical* in line 5?
   (A) fanciful   (B) tiresome
   (C) serious   (D) artificial

   1. _____

2. A *compulsion* (line 13) can best be explained as a(n) _____.
   (A) curved object   (B) sudden, clever plan
   (C) violation of a promise   (D) irresistible impulse

   2. _____

3. Which word or words could best replace *exasperated* in line 14?
   (A) liable to break   (B) greatly annoyed
   (C) elderly   (D) bruised

   3. _____

4. Which word or words could best replace *ironic* in line 20?
   (A) contrary to what might be expected   (B) predominant
   (C) tragic   (D) exceptional

   4. _____

5. Which words could best replace *extirpating* in line 23?
   (A) laughing loudly   (B) rendering fit
   (C) destroying totally   (D) examining carefully

   5. _____

6. Which word or words could best replace *capitulated* in line 24?
   (A) charmed   (B) gave up all resistance
   (C) burdened with trouble   (D) complained fretfully

   6. _____

7. Which word or words could best replace *obscure* in line 31?
   (A) occurring by chance   (B) cutting
   (C) not well known   (D) tentative or restrained

   7. _____

8. Which words could best replace *abstruse* in line 32?
   (A) difficult to understand   (B) being such that alteration is possible
   (C) tolerant in judging others   (D) conforming to current fashion

   8. _____

9. *Ethics* (line 35) can best be explained as _____.
   (A) shortcuts   (B) protective coverings
   (C) a succession of stages   (D) a set of rules or standards

   9. _____

10. *Aficionados* (line 36) can best be described as _____.
    (A) swift, cutting blows   (B) loyal fans
    (C) numbers from which to choose   (D) government authorities

    10. _____

Applying Meaning

Read each sentence below. Write "correct" on the answer line if the vocabulary word has been used correctly. Write "incorrect" on the answer line if the vocabulary word has been used incorrectly.

1. Already late and *exasperated* by the long lines, Ms. Mercato abandoned her full grocery cart at the checkout stand and left the store.

   1. _____

2. The children were *capitulated* by the clowns and the tightrope walkers at the circus.

   2. _____

3. *Ironically*, when I attempted to push Jason off the dock, I slipped and fell into the water myself.

   3. _____

4. Wendy chose an *obscure* American painter from the seventeenth century as the topic of her paper, hoping that she would know more about him than would the teachers who would grade it.

   4. _____

5. To move the house to a new location would require a highly *whimsical* plan.

   5. _____

For each word used incorrectly, write a sentence using the word properly.

_____

_____

_____

_____

_____

_____

_____

_____

_____

_____

_____

Write each sentence below. In the space write a form of the word in parentheses. The form of the word in parentheses may be correct.

6. After trying for so long, Camille was delighted with the _____ of her smoking habit. (extirpate)

_____

_____

_____

7. After the _____ of calculus, Sylvia was actually looking forward to English. (abstruse)

   _____

   _____

   _____

8. Lady Macbeth's _____ hand washing after the murder of Duncan reinforces the theme of guilt in the tragedy. (compulsion)

   _____

   _____

   _____

9. Gordon is a devoted _____ of Frances Parkinson Keyes's work. Not only does he own every novel that Keyes wrote, but he has also visited the writer's childhood home. (aficionado)

   _____

   _____

   _____

10. Frank resigned from the school's shopper network because he decided that it is not _____ to encourage people to buy things for which they have no use. (ethics)

    _____

    _____

    _____

Mastering Meaning

Some subjects, skills, and tasks are more challenging to master than others. Choose something that caused you a problem initially, such as perfecting a high dive, driving a car with manual transmission, or making friends with a new student. Write an essay discussing what caused your difficulty and explaining how you overcame it. Keep in mind that your goal is to inspire others to work hard at meeting the challenges that face them. Use some of the words you studied in this lesson.

Name _____

People's styles of speaking are as varied as their appearances or personalities. While there are probably individuals who can mesmerize you with a well-told story, there may be just as many whose delivery can put you to sleep. The words in this lesson will enable you to express your thoughts about those who have the "gift of gab" as well as those who do not.

Unlocking Meaning

Read the sentences or short passages below. Write the letter for the correct definition of the italicized vocabulary word.

While "Have a nice day" is a considerate way of saying good-bye, constant repetition has turned it into a meaningless *bromide*.

  1. (A) revival of classical literature
  (B) commonplace statement; cliché
  (C) sensitive subject
  (D) place of refuge

Mr. Yonan's *discourse* on opera clearly bored his listeners, who were more interested in rock and roll.

  2. (A) lack of politeness
  (B) respectful attention
  (C) inconvenience
  (D) formal, lengthy discussion

Marguerite will not get her master's degree until she completes and defends her *disquisition* on Sir Max Beerbohm, the British caricaturist, writer, and wit.

  3. (A) formal written discussion
  (B) dramatic role
  (C) architectural plan
  (D) strict rule

If given the opportunity, Daniel will *expatiate* about the wonders of scuba diving in the Caribbean to anyone who will listen.

  4. (A) eject from a position
  (B) speak at length
  (C) ponder reflectively
  (D) ease the agitation of

Words

bromide

discourse

disquisition

expatiate

facetious

prate

prattle

prolixity

raconteur

raillery

1. _____

2. _____

3. _____

4. _____

When Cassie is being *facetious* she can be extremely entertaining. When her friends want to discuss something serious, however, they find her jokes offensive.

5. (A) wild

   (B) peaceful

   (C) humorous

   (D) compassionate

5. _____

Miguel had a tendency to *prate* on about issues he had little knowledge of.

6. (A) talk idly; babble

   (B) keep out of sight

   (C) mention individually

   (D) divide into parts

6. _____

Milo finally told Ms. Santorelli that his partners' *prattle* prevented them from focusing on the history project. He was doing all the real work while they gossiped.

7. (A) slow, easy stroll

   (B) romantic infatuation

   (C) uniform coverage

   (D) meaningless chatter

7. _____

While I admire the works of Henry James, his *prolixity* can be tiring. His use of the stream-of-consciousness technique means that every thought, feeling, and reaction of his characters is recorded in minute detail.

8. (A) change in appearance

   (B) punishment

   (C) wordiness

   (D) extreme poverty

8. _____

Malka is my favorite *raconteur;* even the simplest account of a trip to the mall takes on a new dimension when she narrates it.

9. (A) interpreter

   (B) excellent teller of anecdotes and stories

   (C) protector

   (D) object of affection

9. _____

Dinesh's *raillery* sometimes gets out of hand. When he makes fun of Mark's height or Carmen's braces, you can see them cringe.

10. (A) good-natured teasing

    (B) cooperation

    (C) classical scholarship

    (D) deceptiveness

10. _____

Applying Meaning

Follow the directions below to write a sentence using a vocabulary word.

1. Describe a remark someone might make. Use any form of the word *facetious*.

   _____

   _____

   _____

2. Use the word *discourse* in a sentence about school.

   _____

   _____

   _____

3. Comment on the experience of a baby-sitter in charge of two small children for a week. Use the word *prattle*.

   _____

   _____

   _____

4. Use the word *raillery* in a sentence about the relationship between two people.

   _____

   _____

   _____

Each question below contains a vocabulary word from this lesson. Answer each question "yes" or "no" in the space provided.

5. Should a caller exercise *prolixity* when making an emergency call to the fire department?   5. _____

6. Would a detective conduct a *disquisition* into the circumstances of a serious crime?   6. _____

7. Would a *raconteur* add life to a party?   7. _____

8. Can witty expressions turn into *bromides* after years of overuse?   8. _____

9. If you were in a hurry to get home after school, would you be impatient for your teacher to *expatiate*?   9. _____

10. Is *prating* frowned upon in a study hall?   10. _____

For each question you answered "no," write a sentence using the vocabulary word correctly.

_____

_____

_____

_____

_____

_____

_____

_____

_____

_____

_____

_____

Bonus Word

filibuster

The modern word *filibuster* can be traced to Spanish, French, and Dutch words meaning "freebooter" or "pirate." The English word was originally applied to gunrunners in Central America, but it eventually came to refer to the legislative tactic of making long speeches in order to delay or kill a proposed law. It began to acquire this new meaning after some members of Congress described this tactic as "filibustering" against the United States.

Cooperative Learning: Work in pairs or small groups to brainstorm a list of other political terms, such as *gerrymander, logroll, pork barrel, rubber stamp,* and so forth. Create a glossary of these terms by listing each one alphabetically, writing its current definition, and giving an example of how it is used.

Name _____

The root *-mut-* comes from the Latin word *mutare*, meaning "to change," while the root *-plic-* comes from the Latin word *plicare*, meaning "to fold." Both of these roots appear in a number of English words. For example, if you *mutilate* something, you change it by damaging it. If something is *complicated*, it is "folded" or twisted into many parts. In this lesson you will learn ten words that retain some part of the original Latin.

Root	Meaning	English Word
-mut-	to change	mutate
-plic-	to fold	duplicity

Unlocking Meaning

Write the vocabulary word that fits each clue below. Then say the word and write a short definition. Compare your definition and pronunciation with those given on the flash card.

1. This verb comes from the Latin word *replicare*, meaning "to fold back or repeat." To confirm the results of an experiment, scientist may do this to the process to see if the results are the same.

   Replicate : to duplicate something, make a copy from an original source.

2. This noun begins with the *com-* prefix, and in this word it is attached to the *-plic-* root. It is often used in discussions about crime and guilt.

   Complicity : Helping somebody to do something wrong.

3. This verb combines the prefix *trans-*, meaning "beyond" or "across," and the Latin word *mutare*. Alchemists once tried to do this to lead in the hope of creating gold.

   transmute : a migration in the form or shape to gain more capabilities.

4. This adjective comes from the Latin *explicare*, meaning "to unfold." If you give this type of directions, no one should get lost.

   explicit : Something not clear, something that would be know internally.

Words

commute

complicity

duplicity

explicit

implicit

inexplicable

mutate

permutation

replicate

transmute

5. This adjective comes from the Latin *implicare*, meaning "to entangle." It has the opposite meaning of the answer to number 4.

   Impliit : Something that presents clearly and described completely.

6. This adjective begins with two prefixes. The first means "not" and the second means "out." A literal interpretation of the prefixes and root might be "not able to be folded out." Some might use this word to describe UFOs.

   Inexplicable ; Something that can not be explained are inexplicable.

7. This noun came into English through the Latin *duplicitas*, meaning "doubleness." Perhaps "double-dealing" would be a more accurate translation.

   Duplicity: doing something wrong, doing something again.

8. This noun contains the prefix *per-*, meaning "thoroughly," and the Latin word *mutare*. Dickens's well-known character Scrooge undergoes this when he changes from a miserly grouch to a generous benefactor.

   Mutate: change in nature or shape to gain more capabilities.

9. This word is built from the prefix *com-*, meaning "with," and the root *mutare*. The president or governor might do this to the death sentence of a criminal.

   Commute.

10. This verb comes directly from the Latin word *mutare*, meaning "to change." When genes and chromosomes do this, a disease like sickle cell anemia may result.

    Transumute

Applying Meaning

Read each sentence below. Write "correct" on the answer line if the vocabulary word has been used correctly. Write "incorrect" on the answer line if the vocabulary word has been used incorrectly.

1. Even though he never entered the bank, he was accused of *complicity* in the robbery because he drove the getaway car.

   1. _Correct_

   explicit
2. The *implicit* terms of the lease were clearly stated in the paperwork signed by all parties.

   2. _Incorrect_

3. As an art forger, the painter was able to *replicate* the works of the Old Masters so thoroughly that most people could not detect any difference.

   3. _Correct_

4. After complaining about school for years, Verna felt *inexplicably* sad when she thought about her senior year ending.

   4. _Correct_

5. After weeks at sea with little food and water, the captain feared his crew would *mutate*.

   5. _Incorrect_

   mutiny

For each word used incorrectly, write a sentence using the word properly.

_____

_____

_____

_____

_____

_____

_____

_____

_____

Decide which word in parentheses best completes the sentence. Then write the sentence, adding the missing word.

6. When he discovered the rent check buried beneath a pile of magazines on his desk, the landlord _____ the penalty he had charged Catherine. (commuted; replicated)

_____

_____

_____

7. Miranda did not spend the night at her friend's house as she had told her parents. When her parents learned of her ___, they grounded her for a month. (duplicity; explicitness)

_____

_____

_____

8. The appointment of a new president caused a _____ in the character of the college advisory board. (permutation; replication)

_____

_____

_____

9. Even though the recipe _____ warned not to overcook the fish, Les managed to make the cod tough and dry. (explicitly; inexplicably)

_____

_____

_____

10. The _____ of the ugly duckling into the beautiful swan illustrates how someone can blossom after an unpromising beginning. (duplicity; transmutation)

_____

_____

_____

Cultural Literacy Note

The word *Armageddon* is derived from the biblical prophecy that the final battle between good and evil on Judgment Day will be fought on the battlefield of Armageddon, in modern-day Israel. Today, the word often refers to an all-out nuclear war that marks the end of the world.

Use the Library: The number of words and expressions that have historical connections to war or battle may surprise you. Use a dictionary, an etymological encyclopedia, and other library resources to research the origins and modern definitions of the following words.

blitz	blockbuster	booby trap	brinkmanship
cold war	fail-safe	fallout	flak

Name _____

How well do you remember the words you studied in Lessons 28 through 30? Take the following test covering the words from the last three lessons.

Part 1 Antonyms

Each question below includes a word in capital letters, followed by four words or phrases. Choose the word or phrase that is most nearly <u>opposite</u> in meaning to the word in capital letters. Consider all choices before deciding on your answer. Write the letter for your answer on the line provided.

Sample

S. HIGH	(A) cold	(B) simple	**S.** ___C___
	(C) low	(D) foolish	

1. OBSCURE (A) intentional ✓(B) well-known (C) careless (D) crude   1. _____

2. INEXPLICABLE (A) inescapable ✓(B) explainable (C) huge (D) sincere   2. _____

3. PROLIXITY (A) amateurish (B) boredom ✓(C) brevity (D) seriousness   3. _____

4. WHIMSICAL ✓(A) impulsive (B) fanciful (C) unintentional (D) thoroughly planned   4. _____

5. PRATTLE (A) thoughtful discussion (B) soft surface ✓(C) idle chatter (D) good-natured joke   5. _____

6. DUPLICITY ✓(A) unique appearance (B) feeling of exhaustion (C) honesty (D) unmatchable achievement   6. _____

7. CAPITULATE (A) reorganize (B) compliment (C) reduce in size and importance (D) triumph   7. _____

8. EXASPERATE (A) inflate (B) delight (C) exhaust (D) convert   8. _____

9. EXPLICIT ✓(A) hidden (B) described in depth (C) innocent (D) disorganized   9. _____

Go on to next page. ➤

10. MUTATE   (A) praise   (B) silence completely   **10.** _____
(C) criticize harshly   ✓(D) remain constant

11. EXTIRPATE   (A) condemn   (B) remain pure   **11.** _____
(C) loosen   (D) promote
vigorously

12. ABSTRUSE   (A) well-designed   (B) tiny   **12.** _____
(C) simple   (D) pleasant

13. IRONIC   (A) expected   (B) airy   **13.** _____
(C) portable   (D) smooth

14. BROMIDE   (A) harmless substance   (B) original remark   **14.** _____
(C) cure-all   (D) blame

15. COMPULSION   (A) attraction   (B) obstacle   **15.** _____
(C) self-control   (D) agreement

Part 2 Matching Words and Meanings

Match the definition in Column B with the word in Column A.
Write the letter of the correct definition on the line provided.

Column A   **Column B**

16. raconteur   a. humorous   **16.** _____

17. aficionado   b. involvement in a crime   **17.** _____

18. ethics   c. implied   **18.** _____

19. facetious   d. lessen a penalty   **19.** _____

20. raillery   e. gifted teller of tales   **20.** _____

21. commute   f. rules of conduct   **21.** _____

22. expatiate   g. formal written discussion   **22.** _____

23. implicit   h. teasing   **23.** _____

b. **24.** complicity   i. speak at great length   **24.** _____

25. disquisition j. fan   **25.** _____

Lesson
31
Part A

Name _____

Teetering between Terror and Ecstasy

Words

distraught

genteel

gyrate

harrowing

inexorable

kinetic

masochist

nexus

undulate

visceral

Screams pierce the air as the line of people pushes you **inexorably** toward your destination. Suddenly, it is your turn, and you and your fellow **masochists** climb into the fiberglass cars. As the restraining bar locks in place, you grip it with clammy hands. The mechanical noises that sur-
5 round you cannot drown out the pounding of your heart. Your adrena-line pumps as the train lurches slowly up the hill, deepening the **visceral** feeling that something awful is about to happen. Then it does: at sixty miles an hour, you free-fall down a fifty-five-degree drop. Within two gut-wrenching minutes, you zoom around several loops, **gyrate** through a
10 corkscrew, and shoot like a boomerang into a final loop, pinned to your seat all the while by a force of nearly four times your body weight. Your screams of terror subside as the ride comes to an end. Climbing out of the car, you wobble between fun and fear, happiness and horror. Having survived this **harrowing** experience, you wonder why anybody would have
15 invented the roller coaster.

The concept of the roller coaster probably started with Russian empress Catherine the Great, who had the serfs at her summer palace construct an amusement for her guests. After climbing to a third-story terrace, these oth-erwise **genteel** aristocrats stepped into a compact carriage that sped them
20 screaming down a wooden track. A century later, the Switchback Gravity Pleasure Railway, the first coaster to ride over **undulating** hills, was con-structed on the same principle at Coney Island, New York: attendants pushed railcars up an artificial hill, and gravity took over from there. People have been paying money to be scared witless ever since.

25 The basic principles of roller-coaster design have not changed much. Once the train is pulled up an incline, usually by a simple motor turning a chain, the potential energy is converted into **kinetic** energy, or a con-trolled falling. Today computer-simulated models allow engineers to design coasters with the steepest possible inclines and the most sharply
30 banked curves.

The essential elements of any great roller coaster ride have not changed much either: there must be a **nexus** of startling surprises properly spaced to build tension. The drops, loops, boomerangs, and corkscrews must be good enough to make long waits worthwhile. With names like Shock
35 Wave, Beast, Mindbender, King Cobra, and Vortex, roller coasters have become taller, faster, steeper, and, above all, scarier than they have ever been. Year after year the screams of **distraught** riders attest to the enduring popularity of the roller coaster.

Each word in this lesson's word list appears in dark type in the selection you just read. Think about how the vocabulary word is used in the selection, then write the letter for the best answer to each question.

1. Which word or words could best replace *inexorably* in line 1?   1. _____
   (A) in a dejected way   (B) resourcefully
   (C) steadily and relentlessly (D) proudly

2. A *masochist* (line 3) can best be described as _____.   2. _____
   (A) one who enjoys being hurt (B) one who mistreats others
       or abused
   (C) a deficiency or flaw   (D) a particularly notable person
                                       or thing

3. Which word or words could best replace *visceral* in line 6?   3. _____
   (A) lean and muscular   (B) deeply felt; profound
   (C) causing disaster   (D) joyous

4. Which words could best replace *gyrate* in line 9?   4. _____
   (A) fit closely to the skin   (B) skip or glide
   (C) cut with forceful strokes (D) revolve around a fixed point

5. Which word or words could best replace *harrowing* in line 14?   5. _____
   (A) hasty and careless   (B) glossy
   (C) extremely distressing   (D) playfully mischievous

6. Which word or words could best replace *genteel* in line 19?   6. _____
   (A) polite and refined   (B) impoverished
   (C) insecure   (D) related through marriage

7. Which word or words could best replace *undulating* in line 21?   7. _____
   (A) discolored   (B) wavelike in form
   (C) irritable   (D) straightforward

8. Which words could best replace *kinetic* in line 27?   8. _____
   (A) produced by motion   (B) involving cultural factors
   (C) stationary   (D) expressing concern

9. A *nexus* (line 32) could best be described as a(n) _____.   9. _____
   (A) homogeneous mixture   (B) replacement
   (C) amount spilled   (D) connected series or group

10. Which words could best replace *distraught* in line 37?   10. _____
    (A) showing spite   (B) financially sound
    (C) deeply agitated   (D) readily influenced by suggestion

Applying Meaning

Follow the directions below to write a sentence using a vocabulary word.

1. Describe something that moves. Use any form of the word *kinetic.*

    _____

    _____

    _____

2. Describe a situation involving two people. Use any form of the word *distraught.*

    _____

    _____

    _____

3. Describe an entertainer or dancer. Use any form of the word *gyrate.*

    _____

    _____

    _____

4. Describe the movements of something in nature. Use any form of the word *undulate.*

    _____

    _____

    _____

5. Complete the following sentence: One would have to be a real *masochist* to . . .

    _____

    _____

    _____

Each question below contains a vocabulary word from this lesson. Answer each question "yes" or "no" in the space provided.

6. Would flying through an electrical storm in an airplane be a *harrowing* experience?

    6. _____

7. If you are unable to remove a key from a lock, is the key *inexorable?*

    7. _____

8. When teachers use pictures and charts, are they using *visceral* aids?

    8. _____

9. Is a *nexus* a convenient exit from a large building?

10. Is one expected to behave in a *genteel* manner at a formal dinner?

9. _____

10. _____

For each question you answered "no," write a sentence using the vocabulary word correctly.

_____

_____

_____

_____

_____

_____

_____

_____

_____

_____

_____

_____

_____

_____

_____

_____

_____

_____

Mastering Meaning

Write a descriptive paragraph about your favorite ride at an amusement or water park. Or, if you prefer, describe a ride that you think would be extremely popular at either of these places. In either case, try to use as many senses as possible to bring your experience or idea to life for your readers. Use some of the vocabulary words you studied in this lesson.

Name _____

Do stoplights or rush-hour delays frustrate you? Does the absence of a needed library resource or a favorite shirt send you into a panic? Such situations require words to describe the problem and how we feel about it. In this lesson, you will learn ten words associated with delays or obstructions.

Unlocking Meaning

Read the sentences or short passages below. Write the letter for the correct definition of the italicized vocabulary word.

Because he didn't want to face the mountain of work on his desk, Mr. Brandt chose a *circuitous* route to his office. The trip took longer, but it was much more enjoyable.

1. (A) worthy of respect
   (B) roundabout
   (C) easily forgiven
   (D) precise

In order to *circumvent* the congestion on the Mystic Bridge, Martin decided to take side streets into the city.

2. (A) pass through
   (B) keep watch over
   (C) drift
   (D) bypass; go around

Believe it or not, eating too many carrots can have a *deleterious* effect. After I ate two pounds of them every day for a month, my face and palms appeared to turn a dull shade of orange.

3. (A) harmful
   (B) healthy
   (C) fully conscious
   (D) undisciplined

Rather than going on cholesterol-lowering medication, Dad decided to *eschew* butter, cheese, and red meat.

4. (A) be in readiness
   (B) strike with a hard blow
   (C) avoid habitually
   (D) threaten

Words
circuitous
circumvent
deleterious
eschew
forestall
hiatus
malinger
prevarication
stultify
subterfuge

1. _____

2. _____

3. _____

4. _____

The Hegels *forestalled* the burglary by reporting the man's suspicious behavior to the police.

5. (A) accelerated
    (B) prevented or hindered through certain actions
    (C) observed
    (D) proceeded in an irregular course

5. _____

The strike caused a long *hiatus* in the baseball season, leaving a lot of fans with nothing to talk about.

6. (A) intensity
    (B) justification
    (C) threat
    (D) interruption

6. _____

The supervisor suspected that her new employee might *malinger*, so when he called in sick three days in a row, she demanded he bring a note from his doctor.

7. (A) pretend to be sick in order to avoid a duty
    (B) cause to lose energy
    (C) dilute or weaken
    (D) cause to move back and forth

7. _____

Ronit's continual *prevarication* about her whereabouts on Saturday made her father more suspicious and more determined to learn the truth.

8. (A) weight gain
    (B) personal defect or failing
    (C) cordial greeting
    (D) avoiding the truth; lying

8. _____

Sheila has a habit of making definitive, opinionated statements that tend to *stultify* conversation.

9. (A) firmly reinforce
    (B) have an inhibiting effect on
    (C) exercise authority
    (D) provide entertainment for

9. _____

Jose's attempted *subterfuge* to avoid punishment for breaking the floor lamp never really had a chance. No one believed a kitten could knock over such a heavy item.

10. (A) approximate location
    (B) system of interrelated parts
    (C) deception
    (D) insight

10. _____

Applying Meaning

Decide which word in parentheses best completes the sentence. Then write the sentence, adding the missing word.

1. As soon as the plan for a long hike was announced, a number of _____ began to line up in front of the medical tent. (malingerers; prevarications)

   _____

   _____

   _____

2. Our neighbors hope that by not replacing their broken television set, they will _____ the nightly arguments about which programs to watch. (forestall; prevaricate)

   _____

   _____

   _____

3. The _____ path wound for miles through the forest and ended at the base of the mountain. (circuitous; deleterious)

   _____

   _____

   _____

4. By _____ desserts and fatty foods, Harold has been able to keep his weight at 193 pounds. (eschewing; stultifying)

   _____

   _____

   _____

5. The senators passed their pay raise with a voice vote, employing a _____ to keep their constituents from knowing how they voted on the bill. (hiatus; subterfuge)

   _____

   _____

   _____

Read each sentence below. Write "correct" on the answer line if the vocabulary word has been used correctly. Write "incorrect" on the answer line if the vocabulary word has been used incorrectly.

6. The hurricane forced some international flights to *circumvent* the New York airports and land farther west, in Pittsburgh or Cleveland.

6. _____

7. Many colleges schedule a winter *hiatus* during which students can get valuable work experience by serving as interns.

7. _____

8. An entertaining speaker has a *stultifying* effect on an audience.

8. _____

9. Honesty and trust are *deleterious* to close friendships.

9. _____

10. The prosecutor advised the witness not to *prevaricate* any further and to give only "yes" or "no" answers.

10. _____

For each word used incorrectly, write a sentence using the word properly.

_____

_____

_____

_____

_____

_____

_____

_____

_____

Bonus Word

meander

The ancient Greeks established the city of Miletus at the mouth of the Maeander River (now called the Menderes River) in present-day Turkey. This river twisted and turned repeatedly as it gradually wound its way to the open sea. Our modern word *meander,* meaning "to follow a winding and turning, back-and-forth course," comes from the name of this river. *Meander* is also used in a figurative sense to mean "to move about aimlessly or without purpose."

Cooperative Learning: Our language has many words to describe how one might move from place to place. Work with a partner to write a definition for each of these words. Then try to add other words and definitions to your list.

| sashay | dawdle | scuttle | lope | saunter |

Name _____

The root -*morph*- comes from the Greek word *morphe*, meaning "shape" or "form." When combined with other roots and word parts, it gives us a variety of English words, like *amorphous* and *morpheme*.

The addition of the Greek prefixes *hyper*-, meaning "over" or "above," and *hypo*-, meaning "under" or "below," changes the meaning of roots and words. You see this prefix in words like *hypercritical* and *hypothermia*. The words in this lesson will help you explain concepts that refer to shape as well as those that involve too much or too little of some quality.

Root/ Prefix	Meaning	English Word
-morph-	shape, form	amorphous
hyper-	over, above	hyperbolic
hypo-	under, below	hypochondria

Words
amorphous
hyperbolic
hypercritical
hypersensitive
hyperventilate
hypochondria
hypocrite
hypothermia
hypothesis
morpheme

Unlocking Meaning

Write the vocabulary word that fits each clue below. Then say the word and write a short definition. Compare your definition and pronunciation with those given on the flash card.

1. This noun combines the prefix *hypo*- and a Greek word that means "to suppose." Scientists form one of these before doing an experiment.

   _____

   _____

   _____

2. This adjective comes from the Greek word *huperballein*, meaning "to exceed." This word could be used to describe the statement, "I'm so hungry I could eat a horse."

   _____

   _____

   _____

3. The verb combines the *hyper*- prefix with a root derived from the Latin word *ventus*, meaning "wind." You might do this after great physical exertion or if you are very frightened.

   _____

   _____

   _____

4. This adjective applies to someone who likes to remind others of their faults and shortcomings.

_____

_____

_____

5. This noun combines the prefix _hypo-_ and the Greek word _khondros,_ meaning "cartilage." The ancient Greeks felt that the source of gloom and depression lay under the cartilage of the breastbone.

_____

_____

_____

6. This adjective applies to someone who is easily hurt or offended. This kind of person should stay away from the person described in number 4.

_____

_____

_____

7. This noun came into English through the Latin word _hypocrisis,_ meaning "to act out" or "to play a part." Nowadays it stands for someone who plays a part, but not in the theater.

_____

_____

_____

8. This adjective contains the Greek root _-morph-_ and a prefix that means "without." Clouds blowing across the sky might be described this way.

_____

_____

_____

9. You will find at least one of these "forms" in every word. The word _man_ has one, but _walked_ has two, and _returned_ has three.

_____

_____

_____

10. This noun contains the prefix _hypo-_ and the Greek word for heat, _therme._ Someone lost in the mountains may begin to suffer from this condition.

_____

_____

_____

Applying Meaning

Each question below contains a vocabulary word from this lesson. Answer each question "yes" or "no" in the space provided.

1. Would someone who studies languages be interested in *morphemes*?

1. _____

2. Should *hyperbolic* statements be considered literally true?

2. _____

3. Does it take years of study and hard work to become a *hypochondriac*?

3. _____

4. Would a *hypocrite* say one thing, but then do the opposite?

4. _____

5. Would you offer blankets and a warm drink to someone with *hypothermia*?

5. _____

6. Is the longest side of a right triangle called the *hypothesis*?

6. _____

For each question you answered "no," write a sentence using the vocabulary word correctly.

_____

_____

_____

_____

_____

_____

_____

_____

_____

_____

_____

_____

_____

_____

Follow the directions below to write a sentence using a vocabulary word.

7. Use *hyperventilate* in a sentence about a sporting event.

_____

_____

_____

8. Describe a work of art. Use the word *amorphous*.

_____

_____

_____

9. Use any form of the word *hypercritical* in a sentence about a real or imaginary person.

_____

_____

_____

10. Use any form of the word *hypersensitive* to explain someone's behavior.

_____

_____

_____

Our Living Language

Young people often create novel and colorful expressions that reflect their special interests. Called *slang*, these expressions often are familiar words that have been given new meanings. Slang expressions are rarely accepted into standard English and usually enjoy a brief popularity, then quickly disappear. Some popular slang expressions of the 1960s, for example, include *groovy, far out,* and *right on.*

Cooperative Learning: Work with a partner or in a small group to create a dictionary of current slang terms. Include the pronunciation, definition, and a sample sentence showing how each term is used. You might start with words beginning with *hype-* or *hyper-*. Share some of your words with the class to see if others are familiar with them. Compare your definitions with those of your classmates.

Name _____

How well do you remember the words you studied in Lessons 31 through 33? Take the following test covering the words from the last three lessons.

Part 1 Choose the Correct Meaning

Each question below includes a word in capital letters, followed by four words or phrases. Choose the word or phrase that is <u>closest</u> in meaning to the word in capital letters. Write the letter for your answer on the line provided.

Sample

S. FINISH	(A) enjoy	(B) complete	**S.** ___**B**___
	(C) destroy	(D) enlarge	

1. ESCHEW   (A) pulverize   (B) insist   1. _____
         (C) explain thoroughly   (D) avoid

2. AMORPHOUS   (A) lovable   (B) insulated   2. _____
         (C) without definite shape   (D) meek

3. HIATUS   (A) interruption   (B) sincerity   3. _____
         (C) type of atmosphere   (D) exhaustion

4. MORPHEME   (A) type of medicine   (B) part of a word   4. _____
         (C) stage of development   (D) foolish remark

5. GENTEEL   (A) intelligent   (B) one who is not Jewish   5. _____
         (C) refined   (D) generous

6. UNDULATE   (A) overthrow   (B) weaken or pollute   6. _____
         (C) protect   (D) form waves

7. CIRCUMVENT   (A) go around   (B) ventilate   7. _____
         (C) disfigure   (D) annoy

8. DELETERIOUS   (A) carefree   (B) delicious   8. _____
         (C) harmful   (D) deceitful

9. NEXUS   (A) source of evil   (B) connected series   9. _____
         (C) mystery   (D) microscopic organism

Go on to next page.

Copyright © Glencoe/McGraw-Hill, a division of The McGraw-Hill Companies, Inc.

10. HYPOTHESIS (A) untested assumption (B) exaggerated claim
(C) disease affecting the brain   (D) surgical instrument

10. _____

11. KINETIC (A) peculiar   (B) related by blood
(C) mechanical   (D) having to do with motion

11. _____

12. INEXORABLE (A) relentless   (B) possessed by demons
(C) motionless   (D) unappealing

12. _____

13. HYPERBOLIC (A) geometric   (B) easily fooled
(C) exaggerated   (D) athletic

13. _____

14. PREVARICATION (A) skill in forecasting the future   (B) avoidance of the truth
(C) scandalous behavior   (D) ability to endure hardships

14. _____

15. VISCERAL (A) clearly seen   (B) simple
(C) vicious   (D) deeply felt

15. _____

Part 2 Matching Words and Meanings

Match the definition in Column B with the word in Column A.
Write the letter of the correct definition on the line provided.

Column A	Column B	
16. malinger	a. one who enjoys pain	16. _____
17. hypochondria	b. revolve	17. _____
18. distraught	c. loss of body heat	18. _____
19. stultify	d. fake an illness	19. _____
20. masochist	e. one who is false or insincere	20. _____
21. hypothermia	f. agitated	21. _____
22. circuitous	g. indirect	22. _____
23. subterfuge	h. inhibit	23. _____
24. hypocrite	i. deception	24. _____
25. gyrate	j. irrational concern for one's health	25. _____

Name _____

Shedding Some Light on Light

Isaac Newton, who gave us the three laws of motion, was also fascinated by light. Newton noticed that when a sunbeam passes through a glass prism, the beam of light bends and projects a **spectrum** of colors on a surface. The colors range from red on one end to violet on the other. Newton
5   made a second important observation about light—it is reflected by a mirror in exactly the same way that a ball bounces off a flat surface.

From these observations, Newton hypothesized that light is made up of a variety of multicolored particles and that the particles travel at different speeds, depending on their color. This would explain why a glass prism is
10   able to transform a beam of light into a band of colors. Because each color in the beam travels at a different speed, it bends at a slightly different angle. Hence, the red particles separate slightly from the orange, the orange from the yellow, and so on. Thus, it seemed logical to Newton that the **quintessence** of light is a particle.

15   But then some contradictory observations were made. When light passes through two tiny slits, it bends around the corners of these **apertures**. Furthermore, careful observation revealed that two beams of light can interfere with each other. Particles do not behave this way, but waves do. Further experiments demonstrated that light does indeed have other
20   wave-like properties. So the question arose: Is light made up of particles, waves, or both? This question is such an enigma that scientists have even given the phenomenon a name—wave-particle duality.

Newton and other **devotees** of the particle theory argued that light couldn't be a wave because waves must travel through a medium such as
25   water, and light travels through a vacuum on its way from the Sun to the Earth. To **propitiate** those holding to the particle theory, **proponents** of the wave theory simply decided that there must be some massless, colorless medium that would allow waves to travel through it. Needless to say, many felt such a **flippant** conclusion to be an insult to serious scientific
30   inquiry and treated such **insouciance** with utter disdain.

The issue remained unresolved until a Scottish-born scientist named James Clerk Maxwell (1831–1879) offered a third theory. Because he was not prominently associated with either the particle or the wave theory, Maxwell was able to take a more **dispassionate** look at light, and in doing
35   so proposed that light consists of electromagnetic waves.

So has the issue been settled? Not really. When two sources of light interact, they behave like waves; when light interacts with matter, it behaves like a particle. At present, there seems little hope of **rapprochement** between the two schools of thought on light. For most of us, however, as
40   long as there is light when we flick the switch, it doesn't really matter.

Words

aperture

devotee

dispassionate

flippant

insouciance

propitiate

proponent

quintessence

rapprochement

spectrum

Each word in this lesson's word list appears in dark type in the selection you just read. Think about how the vocabulary word is used in the selection, then write the letter for the best answer to each question.

1. A *spectrum* (line 3) can best be described as a ____.
   (A) type of dye   (B) dull appearance
   (C) theatrical production   (D) wide sequence or range

   1. _____

2. Which words could best replace *quintessence* in line 14?
   (A) essence of something in its purest form   (B) dangerous action
   (C) improper remark   (D) brilliant reflection

   2. _____

3. Which word or words could best replace *apertures* in line 16?
   (A) arrangements   (B) openings
   (C) darkened corners   (D) containers

   3. _____

4. A *devotee* (line 23) is a(n) ____.
   (A) harsh critic   (B) sensible compromise
   (C) ardent supporter or follower   (D) ridiculous idea

   4. _____

5. Which word could best replace *propitiate* in line 26?
   (A) insult   (B) amuse
   (C) ignore   (D) appease

   5. _____

6. Which word could best replace *proponents* in line 26?
   (A) servants   (B) advocates
   (C) critics   (D) relatives

   6. _____

7. A *flippant* (line 29) conclusion is one that is ____.
   (A) made in a thoughtless, offhand manner   (B) revolutionary
   (C) scientifically researched   (D) based on religious beliefs

   7. _____

8. Which words could best replace *insouciance* in line 30?
   (A) careful attention   (B) sweet disposition
   (C) lack of concern   (D) high regard

   8. _____

9. Which word or words could best replace *dispassionate* in line 34?
   (A) accusing   (B) unaffected by facts
   (C) unscientific   (D) impartial; unemotional

   9. _____

10. Which word or words could best replace *rapprochement* in line 38?
    (A) disagreement   (B) reconciliation
    (C) French pastry   (D) violent conflict

    10. _____

Applying Meaning

Follow the directions below to write a sentence using a vocabulary word.

1. Describe a feature of a familiar landscape or building. Use the word *aperture*.

   _____

   _____

   _____

2. Use any form of the word *flippant* in a sentence about a comment someone made.

   _____

   _____

   _____

3. Use *devotee* in a sentence about a belief or interest someone holds.

   _____

   _____

   _____

4. Describe someone's attitude toward an important event. Use any form of the word *insouciance*.

   _____

   _____

   _____

5. Complete the following sentence: The *quintessence* of friendship is . . .

   _____

   _____

   _____

6. Use *rapprochement* in a sentence about the relationship between two countries.

   _____

   _____

   _____

Read each sentence below. Write "correct" on the answer line if the vocabulary word has been used correctly. Write "incorrect" on the answer line if the vocabulary word has been used incorrectly.

7. The *proponents* of the proposed law fought hard for its defeat.

7. _____

8. The chairperson encouraged everyone to speak out because she wanted a broad *spectrum* of ideas available for discussion.

8. _____

9. Because the bus was scheduled to depart in ten minutes, we could not afford to *propitiate* or we would certainly miss it.

9. _____

10. Because the judicial hearing involved the custody of a child, it was difficult to find a *dispassionate* report on the issues.

10. _____

For each word used incorrectly, write a sentence using the vocabulary word properly.

_____

_____

_____

_____

_____

_____

_____

_____

_____

_____

_____

_____

_____

Mastering Meaning

From traffic lights to sunlight, light affects the way you behave and how you live. Write a short personal narrative about a memorable event in your life that involved light or the lack of it. Use some of the words you studied in this lesson.

Lesson
35
Part A

Name _____

The very number of idiomatic expressions for the concepts of concealing and revealing is a good indication of our interest in what is hidden and what is accessible. We value what is revealing, placing importance on an open mind, greeting people with open arms, and maintaining an open-door policy. At the same time, we are intrigued by what is concealed; we unravel the clues of a mystery and seek to explore new worlds. The words in this lesson will help you understand and express these opposing ideas.

Words
blatant
flagrant
flamboyant
flaunt
furtive
obtrusive
recondite
salient
sequester
vestige

Unlocking Meaning

Read the sentences or short passages below. Write the letter for the correct definition of the italicized vocabulary word.

Kathy's *blatant* vanity is rude and inconsiderate. She thinks nothing of removing a mirror from her purse at a restaurant and running a comb through her long, red hair.

1. (A) courageous
   (B) appropriate
   (C) offensively obvious
   (D) dramatically enchanting

Because of the *flagrant* violation of the dress code by a few seniors, students will no longer be able to wear shorts to school during hot weather. Those seniors knew that cutoffs were not permitted, but they chose to wear them anyway.

2. (A) deliberately noticeable
   (B) courageously noble
   (C) imposingly large
   (D) well-established

1. _____

Richard, who usually dresses in a conservative manner, chose a *flamboyant* purple tuxedo, pink shirt, and purple bow tie and cummerbund for the prom.

2. _____

3. (A) poorly adjusted
   (B) dignified
   (C) suitable
   (D) showy

3. _____

Marietta *flaunted* her huge diamond engagement ring, practically waving it in front of her friends until they noticed it.

4. _____

4. (A) treated in a rough way
   (B) showed off in a conspicuous manner
   (C) controlled the use of
   (D) spoiled through ignorance

The young girl's *furtive* glances over her shoulder seemed suspicious to the guard. As he watched on the security camera, the girl stuffed a T-shirt into her bag.

5. (A) sly or secretive

    (B) artificial

    (C) calling for strength

    (D) causing admiration

5. _____

In a neighborhood of stately, old brick homes with broad lawns, the angular ultramodern structure with its gravel yard was *obtrusive*.

6. (A) showing great skill

    (B) having a special function

    (C) extending toward the middle

    (D) undesirably noticeable

6. _____

The professor delivered another *recondite* lecture on macroeconomics. So as not to appear stupid, I pretended to take notes and occasionally nodded my head as though I agreed. I only hope my friend in graduate school can explain it to me later.

7. (A) old-fashioned

    (B) stimulating

    (C) difficult to comprehend

    (D) simple

7. _____

The *salient* point in Alexander's speech was that Buffalo Bill's Wild West Show was a major influence on the popular image of the romantic and exciting Old West.

8. (A) depending on the understanding of others

    (B) prominent

    (C) motivated solely by a desire for money

    (D) composed of segments

8. _____

According to the newspaper, the author plans to *sequester* himself on a horse farm in Virginia while he writes his next legal thriller.

9. (A) withdraw; seclude

    (B) cause to work closely together

    (C) supply in measured amounts

    (D) copy or imitate

9. _____

With the last *vestige* of daylight fading, the captain searched the horizon, hoping to catch sight of land before nightfall.

10. (A) misconception

    (B) tendency to conform to a pattern

    (C) specified point in time

    (D) trace or mark

10. _____

Name _____

Applying Meaning

Decide which word in parentheses best completes the sentence. Then write the sentence, adding the missing word.

1. Having won the lottery, the Ostermeiers _____ their new wealth by purchasing two new cars and a sailboat. (flaunted; sequestered)

_____

_____

_____

2. Martina circled the parking lot seven times before giving up and _____ parking in a space reserved for handicapped drivers. (flagrantly; reconditely)

_____

_____

_____

3. Max's _____ way of barging into conversations and expecting everyone to listen to him has gotten out of hand. (furtive; obtrusive)

_____

_____

_____

4. The demonstrators showed a _____ disregard for the rights of others and blocked all roads both into and out of the airport. (blatant; recondite)

_____

_____

_____

5. I had to read the chapter three times before I discovered the author's _____ points. (salient; flagrant)

_____

_____

_____

Each question below contains a vocabulary word from this lesson. Answer each question "yes" or "no" in the space provided.

6. If you wanted to avoid being noticed in a crowd of people, would you dress in *flamboyant* clothing?

6. _____

7. Would a person's *furtive* manner win him or her instant trust?

7. _____

8. If a person had been *sequestered* for months, would he or she be knowledgeable about recent events?

8. _____

9. Are *recondite* mathematical formulas hard to understand?

9. _____

10. Would burglars try to remove every *vestige* of their presence to avoid getting caught?

10. _____

For each question you answered "no," write a sentence using the vocabulary word correctly.

_____

_____

_____

_____

_____

_____

_____

_____

_____

_____

Our Living Language

The familiar word *clue*, which is so popular in mystery stories, has an ancient derivation. Its ancestor, *clew*, which means "ball," refers primarily to a ball of string or yarn. The mythological Greek hero Theseus had to kill the Minotaur, a monster that had a man's body and a bull's head. Finding the Minotaur in his labyrinth was no problem, but getting out again might have been if the king's daughter had not provided Theseus with a clew of string. Theseus unwound the ball as he entered the maze and wound it up as he returned. Over time, *clue* came to mean a guide to any solution.

Do Some Research: Many of the words associated with mysteries and thrillers have interesting histories. Use a dictionary or etymological encyclopedia to find out the story behind one or more of the words below. Give an oral report on your findings to the class.

| constable | coroner | court | hostage |

Name _____

The Greek prefix *dia-* means "through" or "across"; the Greek prefix *epi-* means "on," "over," or "around." When added to roots or words, these prefixes can change or add to the meaning of the word or root. In this lesson you will learn ten words with one of these two prefixes.

Prefix	Meaning	English Word
dia-	through, across	diatribe
epi-	on, over, around	epidermis

Unlocking Meaning

Write the vocabulary word that fits each clue below. Then say the word and write a short definition. Compare your definition and pronunciation with those given on the flash card.

1. The adjective form of *episode,* this word could describe a type of story.

_____

_____

_____

2. This noun contains the prefix *epi-* and a form of the Greek word *temnein.* When it comes to evil, the devil is this.

_____

_____

_____

3. This noun is built from the prefix *epi-* and the Greek word *taphos,* meaning "tomb." "Rest in peace" is one example of this.

_____

_____

_____

4. This noun originated with the Greek word *diatribein,* meaning "to rub hard." If you were subjected to this, you might well feel you had been "rubbed" the wrong way.

_____

_____

_____

Words

diadem

diametrical

diaphanous

diatribe

epidermis

episodic

epistemology

epitaph

epithet

epitome

5. This noun combines the prefix *epi-* and the Greek word *derma*, meaning "skin." A sunburn would cause this to peel.

_____

_____

_____

6. This noun is built from the prefix *dia-* and the Greek word *dein*, meaning "to bind." A queen might wear this "around" her head to signal her status.

_____

_____

_____

7. This noun comes from the Greek word *epistasthai*, meaning "to understand," and the *-ology* suffix found in words for areas of learning. The word has something to do with learning about learning.

_____

_____

_____

8. You can see the Greek word *phainein*, meaning "to show," in this word. It literally means "show through" and might be used to describe a fabric like gauze.

_____

_____

_____

9. This noun is built from the prefix *epi-* and the Greek word *tithenai*, meaning "to place." This can be an insult or a compliment, as when Lincoln is called the Great Emancipator.

_____

_____

_____

10. This adjective contains the prefix *dia-* and the Greek word *metron*, meaning "measure." This word is often used to describe differing opinions.

_____

_____

_____

Applying Meaning

Read each sentence below. Write "correct" on the answer line if the vocabulary word has been used correctly. Write "incorrect" on the answer line if the vocabulary word has been used incorrectly.

1. Some scientists believe the *epidermis* of the Earth consists of molten lava.

2. Charles Dickens's novels tend to be highly *episodic* because many were published a chapter at a time in monthly magazines.

3. Our visitors from Ireland spoke with such strong *diadems* that I sometimes had difficulty understanding them.

4. Ms. Rostenski chose a *diaphanous* fabric for the curtains so the morning sun would brighten the room.

5. *Epistemology* asks the question "How do we know what we know?"

6. Inscribed on the tomb is the *epitaph* "Here rests in honored glory an American soldier known but to God."

7. Kim felt it was wrong of the coach to *epitomize* her performance in front of the entire team.

1. _____

2. _____

3. _____

4. _____

5. _____

6. _____

7. _____

For each word used incorrectly, write a sentence using the word properly.

_____

_____

_____

_____

_____

_____

_____

_____

_____

_____

_____

_____

_____

_____

Decide which word in parentheses best completes the sentence. Then write the sentence, adding the missing word

8. "Richard the Lionhearted" was a(n) _____ chosen to honor King Richard I of England, a famed warrior. (diadem; epithet)

_____

_____

_____

9. Angry about the broken chair, Grace's mother delivered a(n) _____ about the irresponsibility of teenagers. (diatribe; epistemology)

_____

_____

_____

10. Jacob and his father held _____ opinions about what should be done with the prize money. (diametrical; diaphanous)

_____

_____

_____

Test-Taking Strategies

Analogy tests require you to think carefully about how two words are related and then choose a word pair that best expresses a similar relationship. Begin by analyzing the capitalized words to determine their relationship. Then eliminate the word pairs that have different relationships. Don't be tricked by answer choices that express the desired relationship in reverse.

S. BOVINE:COW::

   (A) deer:antlers   (B) legally:recognized

   (C) canine:dog   (D) feminine:woman

S. _____ **C** _____

Practice: Each question below consists of a related pair of words, followed by four pairs of words or phrases. Select the pair that best expresses the relationship of the original pair.

1. CONTEMPORARY:MODERN::   1. _____

   (A) old:new   (B) high:low

   (C) up-to-date:obsolete   (D) ancient:antique

2. MAESTRO:ORCHESTRA::   2. _____

   (A) commander:army   (B) servant:master

   (C) candidate:politics   (D) head:principal

3. KERNEL:CORN::   3. _____

   (A) nucleus:atom   (B) page:book

   (C) knife:blade   (D) kin:fraternal

Name _____

How well do you remember the words you studied in Lessons 34 through 36? Take the following test covering the words from the last three lessons.

Part 1 *Choose the Correct Meaning*

Each question below includes a word in capital letters, followed by four words or phrases. Choose the word or phrase that is <u>closest</u> in meaning to the word in capital letters. Write the letter for your answer on the line provided.

Sample

S. FINISH	(A) complete	(B) enjoy	S. ____A____
	(C) destroy	(D) enlarge	

1. SALIENT	(A) salty	(B) prominent	1. _____
	(C) attractive	(D) lean	
2. DEVOTEE	(A) villain	(B) scholar	2. _____
	(C) legal proclamation	(D) enthusiast	
3. FLAMBOYANT	(A) flashy	(B) easily ignited	3. _____
	(C) plain	(D) floating readily	
4. FURTIVE	(A) fertile	(B) peculiar	4. _____
	(C) secretive	(D) elaborate	
5. EPITAPH	(A) insult	(B) inscription on a tomb	5. _____
	(C) title	(D) surface	
6. APERTURE	(A) appearance	(B) art expert	6. _____
	(C) harsh criticism	(D) opening	
7. VESTIGE	(A) visible trace	(B) type of garment	7. _____
	(C) wordiness	(D) illegal scheme	
8. EPITOME	(A) large book	(B) edge	8. _____
	(C) example	(D) covered archway	
9. PROPITIATE	(A) pollute	(B) appease	9. _____
	(C) simplify	(D) exaggerate	
10. QUINTESSENCE	(A) witty remark	(B) irritation	10. _____
	(C) solemn mood	(D) purest essence	

Go on to next page. ➤

11. DIAPHANOUS   (A) transparent   (B) deceitful   11. _____
(C) related to the body   (D) geometric

12. RECONDITE   (A) silly   (B) abstruse   12. _____
(C) reflective   (D) theoretical

13. DISPASSIONATE   (A) depressed   (B) furious   13. _____
(C) impartial   (D) biased

14. BLATANT   (A) inflated   (B) tasteless   14. _____
(C) conspicuous   (D) invisible

15. DIATRIBE   (A) crown   (B) primitive lifestyle   15. _____
(C) common expression   (D) bitter attack

Part 2 Matching Words and Meanings

Match the definition in Column B with the word in Column A.
Write the letter of the correct answer on the line provided.

Column A	Column B	
16. obtrusive	a. made up of a series of incidents	16. _____
17. flippant	b. remove; separate	17. _____
18. sequester	c. outer skin	18. _____
19. proponent	d. carefree indifference	19. _____
20. rapprochement	e. undesirably noticeable	20. _____
21. flaunt	f. lacking proper seriousness	21. _____
22. episodic	g. reconciliation	22. _____
23. insouciance	h. wide range	23. _____
24. spectrum	i. supporter	24. _____
25. epidermis	j. show off	25. _____

Dictionary

Pronunciation Guide

Symbol	Example	Symbol	Example
ă	pat	oi	boy
ā	pay	ou	out
âr	care	ŏŏ	took
ä	father	ōō	boot
ĕ	pet	ŭ	cut
ē	be	ûr	urge
ĭ	pit	th	thin
ī	pie	*th*	this
îr	pier	hw	which
ŏ	pot	zh	vision
ō	toe	ə	about, item
ô	paw		

Stress Marks: ′(primary); ′(secondary), as in **dictionary** (dĭk′shə-nĕr′ē)

A

a·bey·ance (ə-**bā**′əns) *n.* Temporary suspension or inactivity. -**a·bey**′**ant,** *adj.*

a·bro·gate (**ăb**′rə-gāt) *v.* -**gat·ed, -gat·ing.** To abolish, repeal, or do away with, especially by authority. -**ab·ro·ga**′**tion,** *n.*

ab·struse (ăb-**strōōs**′, əb-) *adj.* Hard to understand. -**ab·struse**′**ness,** *n.* -**ab·struse**′**ly,** *adv.*

ac·cou·tre·ments (ə-**kōō**′trə-mənts) *n.* Items of equipment, furnishings, or dress.

ac·ro·nym (**ăk**′rə-nĭm′) *n.* A word formed from the first (or first few) letters of a series of other words.

ad hoc (ăd **hŏk**′, **hōk**) *adv.* For one specific purpose and no other. *-adj.* Concerned with one specific purpose.

ad in·fi·ni·tum (ăd ĭn′fə-**nī**′təm) *adv.* and *adj.* Endlessly; without limit; forever.

ad·judge (ă-**jŭj**′) *v.* **1.** To decide or judge by law. **2.** To judge to be; deem; consider.

a·dorn (ə-**dôrn**′) *v.* **1.** To decorate; lend beauty to. **2.** To enhance the distinction or glory of.

af·fa·ble (**ăf**′ə-bəl) *adj.* Easy to talk to; warm and friendly; pleasant. -**af**′**fa·bly,** *adv.* - **af**′**fa·bil**′**i·ty,** *n.*

af·fec·ta·tion (ăf′ĕk-**ta**′shən) *n.* **1.** An artificial behavior that is adopted to impress or deceive others. **2.** Show or pretense.

af·fi·da·vit (ăf′ĭ-**dā**′vĭt) *n.* A written statement made under oath before an authorized official.

a·fi·ci·o·na·do (ə-fĭsh′ē-ə-**nä**′dō, ə-fĭs′ē-, ə-fē′sē-) *n., pl.* -**dos.** An enthusiastic admirer; fan; devotee.

a·gog (ə-**gŏg**′) *adv.* and *adj.* In a state of eager anticipation or excitement.

a·lac·ri·ty (ə-**lăk**′rĭ-tē) *n.* **1.** Eagerness; willingness. **2.** Liveliness; briskness; quickness.

al·lege (ə-**lĕj**′) *v.* -**leged, -leg·ing.** To declare or state, especially without proof. -**al·leged,** *adj.* Supposed. -**al·leg**′**ed·ly,** *adv.*

a·mor·phous (ə-**môr´**fəs) *adj.* **1.** Without definite form; shapeless. **2.** Of no particular kind. **3.** Unorganized. -**a·mor´phous·ly,** *adv.*

a·nath·e·ma (ə-**năth´**ə-mə) *n., pl.*-**mas. 1.** A very strong denunciation; curse. **2.** A person or thing that is hated, reviled, or denounced.

an·o·nym·i·ty (ăn´ə-**nĭm´**ĭ-tē) *n., pl.* -**ties. 1.** The condition of being unknown or unacknowledged. **2.** One who is unknown or unacknowledged.

an·ti·pode (**ăn´**tĭ-pōd´) *n.* An exact opposite.

ap·er·ture (**ăp´**ər-chər) *n.* An opening; hole; gap; slit.

a·poc·ry·phal (ə-**pŏk´**rə-fəl) *adj.* Of doubtful authenticity; probably not true. -**a·poc´ry·phal·ly,** *adv.*

a·pol·o·gist (ə-**pŏl´**ə-jĭst) *n.* A person who defends or justifies something such as an action, doctrine, or institution.

ap·pen·dage (ə-**pĕn´**dĭj) *n.* Something attached or added to a larger or more important thing or being.

ar·a·besque (ăr´ə-**bĕsk´**) *n.* A complex, elaborate design of intertwined scrollwork, foliage, flowers, or other figures.

ar·cha·ic (är-**kā´**ĭk) *adj.* **1.** No longer in common use; old. **2.** Old-fashioned; out-of-date. **3.** Of an earlier time; ancient. -**ar·cha´ic·al·ly,** *adv.*

ar·ro·gate (**ăr´**ə-gāt´) *v.* -**gat·ed, -gat·ing.** To claim or seize without a right to do so. -**ar·ro·ga´tion,** *n.*

a·skew (ə-**skyōō´**) *adv.* or *adj.* Out of the proper position; awry; to one side.

as·sent (ə-**sĕnt´**) *v.* To agree; concur. -*n.* Agreement; consent.

a·sym·met·ri·cal (ā´sĭ-**mĕt´**rĭ-kəl) *adj.* Not the same on either side; lacking balanced proportions. -**a´sym·met´ri·cal·ly,** *adv.*

aus·tere (ô-**stîr´**) *adj.* -**ter·er, ter·est. 1.** Very simple; unadorned. **2.** Severe; stern. **3.** Strict or severe in the way one lives. -**aus·ter´i·ty,** *n.* -**au·stere´ly,** *adv.*

a·ver·sion (ə-**vûr´**zhən, shən) *n.* **1.** A strong dislike. **2.** The object that causes strong dislike.

a·vert (ə-**vûrt´**) *v.* **1.** To keep from happening; prevent; ward off. **2.** To turn away or aside, such as a glance.

ax·i·o·mat·ic (ăk´sē-ə-**măt´**ĭk) *adj.* Of, related to, or like a statement that is universally accepted as true; taken for granted. -**ax´i·om,** *n.*

B

be·he·moth (bĭ-**hē´**məth, **bē´**ə-məth) *n.* Something that is enormous in size and power.

be·rate (bĭ-**rāt´**) *v.* -**rat·ed, rat·ing.** To scold angrily and at length.

bes·ti·al (**bĕs´**chəl, **bēs´**-) *adj.* Having the qualities of a beast; savage; brutal; vile. -**bes´tial·ly,** *adv.* -**bes´ti·al´ i·ty,** *n.*

bla·tant (**blāt´**nt) *adj.* **1.** Offensively conspicuous; very obnoxious. **2.** Disagreeably loud or noisy. -**bla´tant·ly,** *adv.*

bour·geois (bōōr-**zhwä´**, **bōōr´**zhwä´) *adj.* Of, relating to, or characteristic of the middle class and its values. -*n.,* A person belonging to the middle class.

brev·i·ty (**brĕv´**ĭ-tē) *n.* Briefness or conciseness, especially in speech.

bro·mide (brō′mīd′) *n.* A trite or common-place saying; cliché.

bu·col·ic (byo͞o-kŏl′ĭk) *adj.* Relating to the countryside; rural; rustic. **-bu·col′i·cal·ly,** *adv.*

C

ca·bal (kə-băl′) *n.* A small group of people secretly plotting or scheming.

cank·er (kăng′kər) *n.* **1.** An open spreading sore. **2.** Any source of corruption and decay.

ca·pit·u·late (kə-pĭch′ə-lāt′) *v.* **-lat·ed, -lat·ing. 1.** To give up all resistance. **2.** To surrender under prearranged terms or conditions.

carp·ing (kär′pĭng) *adj.* Naggingly or unreasonably critical or complaining. **-carp′ing·ly,** *adv.*

caste (kăst) *n.* A rigid social class distinction based on birth, wealth, rank, or religion.

cas·ti·gate (kăs′tĭ-gāt′) *v.* **-gat·ed, gat·ing.** To criticize severely, especially in public; punish; rebuke.

cause cé·lè·bre (kōz′sā-lĕb′rə) *n., pl.* **causes cé·lè·bres** (kōz′sā-lĕb′rə) An issue that causes controversy and arouses heated debate.

ce·ler·i·ty (sə-lĕr′ĭ-tē) *n.* Swiftness, speed; quickness.

cha·ot·ic (kā-ŏt′ĭk) *adj.* Full of confusion and disorder. **-cha·ot′i·cal·ly.** *adv.*

chas·tise (chăs-tīz′, chăs′-tīz) *v.* **-tised, -tis·ing.** To punish, discipline, or reprimand, usually severely, in order to correct. **-chas·tise′ment,** *n.*

chide (chīd) *v.* **chid·ed** or **chid** (chĭd), **chid·ed** or **chid** or **chid·den** (chĭd′n), **chid·ing.** To scold mildly.

chutz·pah (kho͝ot′spə, ho͝ot′-) *n.* Impudence; nerve; gall.

cir·cu·i·tous (sər-kyo͞o′ĭ-təs) *adj.* Round-about; indirect. **-cir·cu′i·tous·ly,** *adv.* **-cir·cu′i·tous·ness,** *n.*

cir·cum·vent (sûr′kəm-vĕnt′) *v.* **1.** To go around; bypass. **2.** To avoid or evade by trickery; evade.

cog·niz·ant (kŏg′nĭ-zənt) *adj.* Fully aware; informed; conscious.

co·her·ent (kō-hîr′ənt, -hĕr′-) *adj.* Connected in a logical or orderly manner; clearly understood. **-co·her′ent·ly,** adv.

coif·fure (kwä-fyo͝or′) *n.* A hairstyle.

com·mute (kə-myo͞ot′) *v.* **-mut·ed, mut·ing. 1.** To change (a penalty, sentence, punishment, etc.) to one less severe. **2.** To exchange.

com·pen·di·um (kəm-pĕn′dē-əm) *n., pl.* **-di·ums** or **-di·a** (-dē-ə). **1.** A list or collection of items. **2.** A brief complete summary.

com·pla·cent (kəm-plā′sənt) *adj.* Self-satisfied; contented with oneself; smug; unconcerned. **-com·pla′cent·ly,** *adv.* **-com·pla′cen·cy,** *n.*

com·plic·i·ty (kəm-plĭs′ĭ-tē) *n., pl.* **-ties.** Involvement in wrongdoing; state of being an accomplice.

com·pul·sion (kəm-pŭl′shən) *n.* **1.** A strong or irresistible impulse to do something. **2.** The act of forcing or urging. **-com·pul′sive,** *adj.*

con·cord (kŏn′kôrd′, kŏng′-) *n.* Agreement; harmony; peace. **-con·cor′dant,** *adj.*

con·sci·en·tious (kŏn′shē-ĕn′shəs) *adj.* **1.** Guided by one's conscience; scrupulous; honest. **2.** Thorough; painstaking. **-con′sci·en′tious·ly,** *adv.*

con·sen·sus (kən-sĕn′səs) *n.* **1.** General agreement or opinion. **2.** A position or opinion reached by a whole group or by a majority.

con·tro·ver·sy (kŏn′trə-vûr′sē) *n., pl.* **-sies.** A dispute, especially one that leads to much discussion. **-con′tro·ver′sial,** *adj.*

con·ven·tion·al (kən-vĕn′shə-nəl) *adj.* **1.** Following accepted custom or practice. **2.** Conforming to traditional standards. **-con·ven′tion·al·ly,** *adv.*

cor·rob·o·rate (kə-rŏb′ə-rāt′) *v.* **-rat·ed, rat·ing.** To confirm as true by giving additional evidence or proof. **-cor·rob′o·ra·tive,** *adj.*

cor·us·cate (kôr′ə-skāt′, kŏr′-) *v.* **-cat·ed, -cat·ing.** To give off flashes of light; glitter; sparkle. **-cor′us·ca′tion,** *n.*

cre·dence (krēd′ns) *n.* **1.** Acceptance as true or real. **2.** Trustworthiness.

cred·i·bil·i·ty (krĕd′ə-bĭl′ĭ-tē) *n.* **1.** The quality or power to inspire belief. **2.** A capacity for belief.

cred·u·lous (krĕj′ə-ləs) *adj.* Tending to believe or trust too readily; gullible. **-cred′u·lous·ly,** *adv.*

crux (krŭks, krŏŏks) *n., pl.* **crux·es** or **cru·ces** (krŏŏ′sēz). The basic, essential, or most important point.

D

dal·ly (dăl′ē) *v.* **-lied, -ly·ing, -lies. 1.** To waste time; dawdle; linger. **2.** To flirt.

de·bil·i·tate (dĭ-bĭl′ĭ-tāt′) *v.* **-tat·ed, -tat·ing.** To weaken; to lessen the strength or energy of. **-de·bil′i·ta′tion,** *n.* **-de·bil′i·ta′tive,** *adj.*

def·er·en·tial (dĕf′ə-rĕn′shəl) *adj.* Showing courteous respect or regard; respectful. **-def′er·en′tial·ly,** *adv.*

del·e·ter·i·ous (dĕl′ĭ-tîr′ē-əs) *adj.* Harmful; injurious; hurtful. **-del′e·ter′i·ous·ly,** *adv.* **-del′e·ter′i·ous·ness,** *n.*

de·mur (dĭ-mûr′) *v.* **-murred, -mur·ring. 1.** To object; show disapproval. **2.** To delay. *-n.* **1.** An objection. **2.** Delay.

de·nom·i·na·tion (dĭ-nŏm′ə-nā′shən) *n.* **1.** A particular religious group. **2.** A unit in a series of numbers, kinds, values, or sizes. **3.** A name.

de·plore (dĭ-plôr′, -plōr′) *v.* **-plored, -plor·ing. 1.** To regret deeply. **2.** To disapprove of strongly. **-de·plor′a·ble,** *adj.*

dep·re·cate (dĕp′rĭ-kāt′) *v.* **-cat·ed, -cat·ing. 1.** To express disapproval of. **2.** To belittle. **-dep′re·ca·to′ry, -dep′re·ca′tive**(-kā′tĭv), *adj.*

de·pre·ci·ate (dĭ-prē′shē-āt) *v.* **-at·ed, -at·ing. 1.** To lessen the value of. **2.** To belittle.

de·rog·a·tor·y (dĭ-rŏg′ə-tôr′ē, -tōr′ē) *adj.* Belittling; expressing a low opinion.

dev·o·tee (dĕv′ə-tē′, -tā′) *n.* One who is enthusiastically devoted to something.

di·a·dem (dī′ə-dĕm′, -dəm) *n.* **1.** A crown. **2.** An ornamental or cloth headband.

di·a·met·ri·cal (dī′ə-mĕt′rĭ-kəl) *adj.* Directly opposite; contrary. **-di′a·met′ri·cal·ly,** *adv.*

di·aph·a·nous (dī-ăf′ə-nəs) *adj.* **1.** Very sheer; transparent. **2.** Airy. **-di·aph′a·nous·ly,** *adv.*

di·a·tribe (dī′ə-trīb′) *n.* A bitter, abusive, often lengthy criticism or denunciation.

di·dac·tic (dī-dăk′tĭk) *adj.* **1.** Intended for instruction. **2.** Morally instructive. **-di·dac′ti·cism,** *n.*

dif·fi·dent (dĭf′ĭ-dənt, -dĕnt) *adj.* Lacking self-confidence; shy; timid.

dil·et·tante (dĭl′ĭ-tänt′, dĭl′ĭ-**tänt**′) *n. pl.,* **-tantes,** also **-tan·ti** (-**tän**′te, -**tăn**′-). A person who dabbles in a field of knowledge for amusement.

dis·ap·pro·ba·tion (dĭs-ăp′rə-**bā**′shən) *n.* Disapproval; condemnation.

dis·course (dĭs′kôrs′, -kōrs) *n.* **1.** A formal speech or discussion of a subject. **2.** Conversation. *-v.* **1.** To speak or write formally. **2.** To converse.

dis·par·age (dĭ-spăr′ĭj) *v.* **-aged, -ag·ing. 1.** To belittle; decry. **2.** To lower in reputation; discredit.

dis·pas·sion·ate (dĭs-păsh′ə-nĭt) *adj.* Not affected by bias or strong feeling; unemotional; impartial. **-dis·pas′sion·ate·ly,** *adv.*

dis·qui·si·tion (dĭs′kwĭ-**zĭsh**′ən) *n.* A formal inquiry into or discussion of a subject.

dis·sent (dĭ-sĕnt′) *v.* To disagree. *-n.* Disagreement; difference of opinion.

dis·so·lu·tion (dĭs′ə-lōō′shən) *n.* **1.** A breaking up into parts; disintegration. **2.** An ending.

dis·suade (dĭ-swād′) *v.* **-suad·ed, -suad·ing.** To discourage (a person) from an action by persuasion or advice.

dis·traught (dĭ-strôt′) *adj.* Deeply agitated; very upset. **-dis·traught′ly,** *adv.*

du·plic·i·ty (dōō-plĭ′sĭ-tē, dyōō-) *n. pl.* **-ties.** Deliberate deceitfulness; double-dealing.

E

é·clat (ā-klä′, ā′-klä) *n.* **1.** Brilliance. **2.** Great praise; acclaim. **3.** A brilliant success or effect.

ed·i·fy (ĕ′de-fī) *v.* **-fied, fy·ing.** To instruct, especially morally, spiritually, or intellectually.

ef·fete (ĭ-fēt′) *adj.* **1.** Having lost character, vitality, or strength. **2.** Marked by self-indulgence or decadence. **ef·fete′ly,** *adv.* **-ef·fete′ness,** *n.*

ef·fi·ca·cy (e′fĭ-kə-sē) *n.* Power to produce the desired results; effectiveness.

e·gal·i·tar·i·an (ĭ-găl′ĭ-**târ**′ē-ən) *adj.* Characterized by belief in equal political, economic, social, and civil rights for all people.

e·gress (e′grĕs′) *n.* **1.** The act of going out. **2.** An exit. **3.** The right of going out. *-v.* To go out.

e·lite (ĭ-lēt′, ā-lēt′) *n., pl.* **e·lite** or **e·lites.** The best, finest, or most powerful members of a group or society. **-e·lite′,** *adj.*

en·gen·der (ĕn-jĕn′dər) *v.* To bring into being; cause; produce.

en·nui (ŏn-wē′, ŏn′wē) *n.* A feeling of listlessness, weariness, or discontent resulting from inactivity or lack of interest; boredom.

en·trance (ĕn-trăns′) *v.* **-tranced, -tranc·ing.** To fill with wonder or delight; enchant; charm.

e·num·er·ate (ĭ-noo′mə-rāt′, ĭ-nyoo′-) *v.* **-at·ed, at·ing.** To name one by one; list. **-e·nu′mer·a′tion,** *n.*

ep·i·der·mis (ĕp′ĭ-dûr′mĭs) *n.* The outermost layer of skin in animals with backbones.

ep·i·sod·ic (ĕp′ĭ-sŏd′ĭk) *adj.* **1.** Having the nature of an incident in a series of events. **2.** Made up of a series of episodes.**-ep′i·sod′ic·al·ly,** *adv.*

e·pis·te·mol·o·gy (ĭ-pĭs′tə-mŏl′ə-jē) *n.* The branch of philosophy in which the nature of human knowledge and its limits are studied.

ep·i·taph (ĕp′ĭ-tăf′) *n.* A brief inscription on a tombstone in memory of the person buried there.

ep·i·thet (ĕp′ə-thĕt′) *n.* A descriptive word or phrase used with or in place of a name to characterize a person or thing.

e·pit·o·me (ĭ-pĭt′ə-mē) *n.* A typical or ideal example. **-e·pit′o·mize,** *v.*

e·qui·poise (e′kwə-poiz′, ĕk′wə-) *n.* A state of balance; equilibrium.

es·chew (ĕs-choo) *v.* To avoid habitually; shun.

eth·ics (ĕth′ĭks) *pl. n. (used with a sing. or pl. verb)* The rules or standards of conduct for an individual or group. **-eth′i·cal,** *adj.*

ex·as·per·ate (ĭg-zăs′pə-rāt′) *v.* **-at·ed, -at·ing.** To make very angry; irritate or annoy greatly. **-ex·as′per·at′ing·ly,** *adv.* **-ex·as′per·at′ed·ly,** *adv.*

ex·hort (ĭg-zôrt) *v.* To urge strongly or earnestly by advice, appeal, argument, or warning.

ex·pa·ti·ate (ĭk-spā′shē-āt′) *v.* **-at·ed, -at·ing.** To speak or write at length or in detail. **-ex·pa′ti·a′tion,** *n.*

ex·pend·a·ble (ĭk-spĕn′də-bəl) *adj.* **1.** Not absolutely necessary. **2.** Capable of being used up. **3.** Capable of being sacrificed to gain an objective.

ex·plic·it (ĭk-splĭs′ĭt) *adj.* Clearly stated; definite. **-ex·plic′it·ly,** *adv.* **-ex·plic′it·ness,** *n.*

ex·tir·pate (ĕk′stər-pāt′) *v.* **-pat·ed, -pat·ing. 1.** To destroy completely. **2.** To pull up by the roots. **-ex·tir·pa′tion,** *n.*

ex·tol (ĭk-stōl′) *v.* **-tolled, -tol·ling.** To praise highly.

F

fa·ce·tious (fə-se′shəs) *adj.* Humorous; playfully joking. **-fa·ce′tious·ly,** *adv.* **-fa·ce′tious·ness,** *n.*

fac·ile (fas′əl) *adj.* **1.** Working or doing with skill and ease. **2.** Easily done. **-fac′ile·ly,** *adv.* **-fac′ile·ness,** *n.*

fac·ti·tious (făk-tĭsh′əs) *adj.* Not natural or real; artificial. **-fac·ti′tious·ly,** *adv.*

fal·la·cy (făl′ə-sē) *n., pl.* **-cies.** A false or mistaken belief or notion; misconception. **-fal·la′cious,** *adj.*

fas·tid·i·ous (fă-stĭd′ē-əs, fə-) *adj.* **1.** Showing careful attention to detail. **2.** Hard to please; exacting. **-fas·tid′i·ous·ly,** *adv.*

fe·al·ty (fē′əl-tē) *n., pl.* **-ties. 1.** Loyalty; faithfulness; allegiance. **2.** The loyalty of a vassal or feudal tenant to his lord.

fea·si·ble (fē′zə-bəl) *adj.* **1.** Capable of being done or carried out; possible. **2.** Suitable. **3.** Likely. **-fea′si·bly,** *adv.* **-fea′si·bil′i·ty,** *n.*

fe·line (fē′līn′) *n.* An animal of the cat family, such as a cat, leopard, lion, or tiger. *-adj.* **1.** Characteristic of a cat or cat family. **2.** Catlike.

fi·du·ci·ar·y (fĭ-**doo**ʹshē-ĕrʹē, -shĕ-rē) *adj.* Relating to the management of one person's assets by another. *-n.* One with such responsibility.

fil·i·gree (**fĭl**ʹĭ-grēʹ) *n.* An intricate, delicate ornamentation. *-adj.* Composed of or like filigree. *-v.* **-greed, -gree·ing.** To decorate with filigree.

fla·grant (**flā**ʹgrənt) *adj.* Openly and offensively bad, wrong, or scandalous; outrageous.

flam·boy·ant (flăm-**boi**ʹənt) *adj.* **1.** Showy; ornate. **2.** Brilliant in color or form. **-flam·boy**ʹ**ance,** *n.* **-flam·boy**ʹ**ant·ly,** *adv.*

flaunt (flŏnt) *v.* To show off in order to impress others; to exhibit shamelessly.

flip·pant (**flĭp**ʹənt) *adj.* Not having or showing the proper respect or seriousness; impertinent; saucy. **-flip**ʹ**pan·cy,** *n.* **-flip**ʹ**pant·ly,** *adv.*

fore·stall (fôr-**stŏl**ʹ, fōr-) *v.* **1.** To prevent or hinder by doing something beforehand. **2.** To anticipate.

fu·ga·cious (fyoo-**ga**ʹshəs) *adj.* Passing away quickly; fleeting. **-fu·ga**ʹ**cious·ly,** *adv.* **-fu·ga**ʹ**cious·ness,** *n.*

func·tion·al (**fŭngk**ʹshə-nəl) *adj.* **1.** Designed for a particular use, duty, or activity. **2.** Capable of performing.

fur·tive (**fûr**ʹtĭv) *adj.* **1.** Done or acting in a stealthy manner; sneaky. **2.** Shifty; sly. **-fur**ʹ**tive·ly,** *adv.*

fu·sil·lade (**fyoo**ʹsə-lād, **-lād**ʹ, zə-) *n.* **1.** A rapid and continuous outburst. **2.** A rapid and continuous firing from a number of firearms.

G

ge·ne·al·o·gy (jēʹnē-**ŏl**ʹə-jē, **-ă**ʹ-, jĕnʹē-) *n., pl.* **-gies. 1.** A record of a family's ancestry. **2.** The study of a family's ancestry and history.

gen·teel (jĕn-**tēl**ʹ) *adj.* **1.** Polite in manner; refined. **2.** Elegant; stylish. **-gen·teel**ʹ**ly,** *adv.*

ge·nus (**jē**ʹnəs) *n., pl.* **gen·er·a.** (**jĕn**ʹər-ə) **1.** A classification of plants and animals having common characteristics. **2.** A class; kind; group; sort.

ger·mi·nal (**jûr**ʹmə-nəl) *adj.* In the first or earliest stage of development. **-ger**ʹ**mi·nal·ly,** *adv.*

gla·brous (**glā**ʹbrəs) *adj.* Without hair; smooth; bald. **-gla**ʹ**brous·ness,** *n.*

glean (glēn) *v.* To collect little by little or gradually. **-glean**ʹ**ings,** *pl. n.*

Goth·ic (**gŏth**ʹĭk) *adj.* Of a style of architecture developed in Europe between the 12th and 16th centuries, characterized by pointed arches and steep roofs.

guise (gīz) *n.* **1.** Outward appearance; semblance. **2.** A false appearance; pretense.

gy·rate (**ji**ʹrāt ʹ) *v.* **rat·ed, rat·ing.** To move in a circle or spiral; rotate around an axis; whirl. **-gy·ra**ʹ**tion,** *n.*

H

hal·cy·on (**hăl**ʹsē-ən) *adj.* Calm; peaceful; happy. *-n.* A kingfisher.

har·row·ing (**hăr**ʹō-ĭng) *adj.* Extremely frightening; distressing; agonizing.

hei·nous (**hā**ʹnəs) *adj.* Extremely wicked or evil; abominable; hateful. **-hei**ʹ**nous·ly,** *adv.*

hi·a·tus (hī-**ā**ʹtəs) *n., pl.* **-tus·es** or **-hiatus.** A break, interruption, or gap in space, time, or continuity.

hom·o·nym (hŏm′ə-nĭm′, hō′mə-) *n.* A word that has the same pronunciation as another word but has a different meaning and spelling.

hy·per·bol·ic (hī′pər-bŏl′ĭk) *adj.* Of, relating to, or using a figure of speech that consists of an extreme exaggeration. **-hy′per·bol′ ic·al·ly,** *adv.*

hy·per·crit·i·cal (hī′pər-krĭt′ĭ-kəl) *adj.* Excessively critical; fault-finding. **-hy′per·crit′i·cal·ly,** *adv.*

hy·per·sen·si·tive (hī′pər-krĭt′ĭ-kəl) *adj.* Highly or excessively sensitive. **-hy′per·sen′si·tive·ness, -hy′per·sen′si·tiv′i·ty,** *n.*

hy·per·ven·ti·late (hī′pər-vĕn′tl-āt) *v.* **-lat·ed, -lat·ing.** To breathe abnormally fast or deeply, as from excitement or anxiety. **-hy′per·ven′ti·la′tion,** *n.*

hy·po·chon·dri·a (hī′pə-kŏn′drē-ə) *n.* A state of anxiety regarding one's health, often with imaginary illnesses. **-hy′po·chon′dri·ac,** *n.* One who suffers from hypochondria.

hyp·o·crite (hĭp′ə-krĭt) *n.* A person who claims to have virtues, beliefs, or feelings that he or she does not have.

hy·po·ther·mi·a (hī′pə-thûr′mē-ə) *n.* A body temperature that is abnormally low. **-hy′po·ther′mic,** *adj.*

hy·poth·e·sis (hī-pŏth′ĭ-sĭs) *n., pl.* **-ses** (-sēz′). An unproved explanation; an assumption; a theory.

I

ig·no·min·y (ĭg′nə-mĭn′ē, -mə-nē) *n., pl.* **-ies.** **1.** Dishonor; shame; disgrace; humiliation. **2.** Disgraceful or shameful act, quality, or behavior.

im·bro·gli·o (ĭm-brōl′yō) *n., pl.* **-glios. 1.** A confusing or complicated situation. **2.** A confused or complicated disagreement.

im·per·ti·nent (ĭm-pûr′tn-ənt) *adj.* **1.** Boldly rude or forward; insolent. **2.** Not relating to the matter at hand; irrelevant.

im·per·turb·a·ble (ĭm′pər-tûr′bə-bəl) *adj.* Not easily disturbed or upset; unshakably calm. **-im′per·turb′a·bly,** *adv.*

im·pe·tus (ĭm′pĭ-təs) *n., pl.* **-tus·es.** The driving force or impulse; stimulus.

im·plic·it (ĭm-plĭs′ĭt) *adj.* Suggested or understood, but not directly expressed. **-im·plic′it·ly,** *adv.* **-im·plic′it·ness,** *n.*

im·preg·na·ble (ĭm-prĕg′nə-bəl) *adj.* **1.** Impossible to capture or take by force; unconquerable. **2.** Unyielding.

in·ad·ver·tent (ĭn′əd-vûr′tnt) *adj.* **1.** Unintentional; accidental. **2.** Not attentive; heedless. **-in′ad·ver′tent·ly,** *adv.*

in·censed (ĭn-sĕnsd′) *v.* Past tense and past participle of **in·cense.** Made very angry; infuriated.

in·cise (ĭn-sīz) *v.* **-cised, cis·ing.** *v.* **1.** To engrave; carve. **2.** To cut into with a sharp tool.

in·con·tro·vert·i·ble (ĭn kon ′ trə vur′tə-bəl) *adj.* Impossible to dispute or debate; unquestion-able; certain. **-in′con·tro·vert′i·bly,** *adv.*

in·di·gent (ĭn′dĭ-jənt) *adj.* Poor; needy. *n.* A needy or poor person. **-in′di·gent·ly,** *adv.*

in·do·lent (ĭn′də-lənt) *adj.* Disliking or avoiding work; lazy; idle. **-in′do·lent·ly,** *adv.*

in·ert (ĭn-ûrt′) *adj.* **1.** Without power to move, act, or resist. **2.** Sluggish; slow; inactive. **-in·ert′ly,** *adv.* **-in·ert′ness,** *n.*

in·ex·o·ra·ble (ĭn-ĕk′sər-ə-bəl) *adj.* **1.** Persistent and steady. **2.** Unrelenting; unyielding; inflexible. **-in·ex′o·ra·bly,** *adv.*

in·ex·plic·a·ble (ĭn-ĕk′splĭ-kə-bəl, ĭn′ĭk-splĭk′ə-bəl) *adj.* Difficult or impossible to explain or understand. **-in·ex′plic·a·bly,** *adv.*

in·fal·li·ble (ĭn-făl′ə-bəl) *adj.* **1.** Incapable of making a mistake; never wrong. **2.** Reliable; dependable. **-in·fal′li·bly,** *adv.*

in·gress (ĭn′grĕs′) *n.* **1.** The act of entering. **2.** An entrance. **3.** The right to enter.

in·sen·sate (ĭn-sĕn′sāt′, -sĭt) *adj.* **1.** Without sensation; inanimate. **2.** Without feeling or sensitivity. **3.** Foolish. **-in·sen′sate·ly,** *adv.*

in·sin·u·a·tion (ĭn-sĭn′yōō-ā′shən) *n.* An indirect suggestion or hint, especially against someone. **-in·sin′u·at·ing,** *adj.*

in·sou·ci·ance (ĭn-sōō′sē-əns, än′sōō-syäns′) *n.* Complete lack of concern; nonchalance; indifference. **-in·sou′ci·ant,** *adj.*

in·su·lar·i·ty (ĭn′sə-lăr′ĭ-tē) *n.* **1.** The state of living on or being an island. **2.** Narrowness of viewpoint. **3.** Isolation.

in·ter·ro·gate (ĭn-tĕr′ə-gāt′) *v.* **-gat·ed, -gat·ing.** To ask questions of a person formally or officially. **-in·ter′ro·ga′tion,** *n.*

in·trep·id (ĭn-trĕp′ĭd) *adj.* Very brave; courageous; fearless. **-in·trep′id·ly,** *adv.* **-in·trep′id·ness,** *n.*

in·tu·i·tive (ĭn-tōō′ĭ-tĭv, -tyōō′-) *adj.* Known or perceived without conscious reasoning. **-in·tu′i·tive·ly,** *adv.*

in·vec·tive (ĭn-vĕk′tĭv) *n.* A violent verbal attack; abusive language. *-adj.* Of, relating to, or characterized by abusive language.

i·ron·ic (ī-rŏn′ĭk) also **-i·ron·i·cal** (ī-rŏn′ĭ-kəl) *adj.* Directly opposite in form to what is expected, expressed, or intended. **-i·ron′i·cal·ly,** *adv.*

J-K-L

jug·ger·naut (jŭg′ər-nôt) *n.* **1.** An overpowering force that destroys anything in its path. **2.** Anything to which people blindly devote themselves.

ki·net·ic (kĭ-nĕt′ĭk, kī-) *adj.* Of, resulting from, or produced by motion. **-ki·net′ic·al·ly,** *adv.*

lan·guor (lăng′gər, lăng′ər) *n.* Listlessness; a quality of dreamy laziness. **-lan′guor·ous,** *adj.*

le·thar·gic (lə-thär′jĭk) *adj.* Sluggish, inactive, or apathetic. **-le·thar′gi·cal·ly,** *adv.*

lis·some (lĭs′əm) *adj.* Supple; flexible; limber; agile. **-lis′some·ly,** *adv.*

M

ma·lin·ger (mə-lĭng′gər) *v.* To pretend to be ill or to have some other incapacity in order to avoid work or duty; shirk. **-ma·lin′ger·er,** *n.*

mal·ver·sa·tion (măl′vər-sā′shən) *n.* Misconduct in public office or other position of trust.

mas·o·chist (măs′ə-kĭst) *n.* A person who gets pleasure from being hurt, punished, embarrassed, or mistreated. **-mas′o·chis′tic,** *adj.*

mé·lange (mā-länzh′) *n.* A mixture; medley.

me·ton·y·my (mə-tŏn′ə-mē) *n., pl.* **-mies.** The substitution of one word or phrase for another with which it is closely associated.

mis·cre·ant (mĭs′krē-ənt) *n.* **1.** A wicked person; villain. **2.** Heretic; one who dissents from church dogma. **-mis′cre·ant,** *adj.*

mis·no·mer (mĭs-nō′mər) *n.* **1.** A name that is unsuitable or unfitting. **2.** A wrong name. **-mis·no′mered,** *adj.*

mod·est (mŏd′ĭst) *adj.* **1.** Having a humble opinion of one's own value, talents, etc. **2.** Free from showiness. **3.** Not extreme. **-mod′est·ly,** *adv.*

mor·pheme (môr′fēm) *n.* The smallest unit of language, such as a word, a root, or an affix, that cannot be divided into smaller meaningful parts.

mu·nif·i·cent (myōō-nĭf′ĭ-sənt) *adj.* Very generous in giving. **-mu·nif′i·cence,** *n.* **-mu·nif′i·cent·ly,** *adv.*

mu·tate (myōō′tāt, myōō-tāt′) *v.* **-tat·ed, -tat·ing.** To change, undergo change, or cause to undergo change in form, nature, or quality.

mys·tique (mĭ-stēk′) *n.* An air of mystery surrounding someone or something.

N

na·bob (nā′bŏb) *n.* A rich, powerful, and influential person.

nex·us (nĕk′səs) *n. pl.* **nexus** or **-us·es. 1.** A connected group or series. **2.** A connection, tie, or link. **3.** The core or center.

no·men·cla·ture (nō′mən-klā′chər, nō-men′klə-) *n.* a system of names or terms used in a branch of learning, such as art or science.

nom·i·nal (nŏm′ə-nəl) *adj.* **1.** Existing in name only, not in fact. **2.** Small in comparison to the actual value. **-nom′i·nal·ly,** *adv.*

O

o·be·i·sance (ō-bā′səns, ō-bē′-) *n.* A bodily gesture, such as a bow or curtsy, that shows respect, homage, or reverence.

ob·scure (ŏb-skyōōr′, əb-) *adj.* **-scur·er, -scur·est. 1.** Not famous; not well known. **2.** Not easily understood. **3.** Not easily noticed. **-ob·scure′ly,** *adv.*

ob·se·qui·ous (ŏb-se′kwē-əs, əb-) *adj.* Excessively willing to serve or obey; fawning. **-ob·se′qui·ous·ness,** *n.*

ob·tru·sive (ŏb-trōō′sĭv, -zĭv, əb-) *adj.* **1.** Undesirably noticeable. **2.** Tending to push or impose oneself on others. **-ob·tru′sive·ness,** *n.* **-ob·tru′sive·ly,** *adv.*

ob·verse (ŏb-vûrs′, əb-, ŏb′vûrs) *n.* **1.** The side of a coin or medal that bears the main design. **2.** The main side of something. *-adj.* Facing the observer.

o·di·ous (ō′dē-əs) *adj.* Causing hatred, aversion, or disgust; offensive. **-o′di·ous·ly,** *adv.*

of·fal (ô′fəl, ŏf′əl) *n.* **1.** Waste parts, especially of a butchered animal. **2.** Rubbish; garbage.

of·fi·cious (ə-fĭsh′əs) *adj.* Too eagerly offering unwanted services or advice. **-of·fi′cious·ly,** *adv.*

om·nis·cient (ŏm-nĭsh′ənt) *adj.* Knowing everything. **-om·nis′cience,** *n.* **-om·nis′cient·ly,** *adv.*

P

pa·cif·ic (pə-sĭf′ĭk) *adj.* **1.** Of a peaceful nature; tranquil; calm. **2.** Tending to diminish conflict. **-pa·cif′i·cal·ly,** *adv.*

pa·lav·er (pə-lăv′ər, -lä′vər) *n.* Idle talk; chatter. *-v.* To talk idly; to chatter.

pal·pa·ble (păl′pə-bəl) *adj.* Easily perceived or noticed; obvious; perceptible. **-pal′pa·bil′i·ty,** *n.* **-pal′pa·bly,** *adv.*

par·a·noid (păr′ə-noid′) *adj.* Characterized or affected by extreme fear or distrust of others.

par·a·phrase (păr′ə-frāz′) *v.* **-phrased, -phras·ing.** To restate in other words while keeping the same meaning. *-n.* A restatement in different words.

par·ti·san (păr′tĭ-zən) *n.* A fervent supporter of a cause or person. *-adj.* Devoted to or biased in favor of a party, cause, or group.

pat·i·na (păt′n-ə, pə-tē′nə) *n.* A change in appearance resulting from continued behavior, practice, or use.

pa·tron·iz·ing (pā′trə-nīz′ĭng) *adj.* Characterized by a superior or condescending manner. **-pa′tron·iz′ing·ly,** *adv.*

pen·chant (pĕn′chənt) *n.* A strong liking or fondness.

pen·sive (pĕn′sĭv) *adj.* In deep and serious, often dreamy, thought. **-pen′sive·ly,** *adv.*

per·fid·i·ous (pər-fĭd′-ē-əs) *adj.* Treacherous; disloyal; faithless. **-per·fid′i·ous·ly,** *adv.*

per·mu·ta·tion (pûr′ myoo-tā′shən) *n.* a complete change, alteration, or transformation.

per·pend (pər-pĕnd′) *v.* To think about carefully; ponder; reflect.

per·so·na non gra·ta (pər-sō′nə nŏn grä′tə, grăt′ə) *adj.* Being unacceptable or unwelcome. *-n.* A person who is not acceptable or not welcome.

per·verse (pər-vûrs′, pûr′vûrs) *adj.* **1.** Turned away from what is right, good, reasonable, or acceptable; wicked. **2.** Stubborn. **-per·verse′ly,** *adv.*

phi·lip·pic (fĭ-lĭp′ĭk) *n.* A bitter verbal attack or condemnation.

phleg·mat·ic (flĕg-măt′ĭk) *adj.* Difficult to rouse to action; calm; unemotional; indifferent; apathetic. **-phleg·mat′ic·al·ly,** *adv.*

phys·i·og·no·my (fĭz′ē-ŏg′nə-mē, -ŏn′ə-mē) *n., pl.* **-mies. 1.** The face; facial features. **2.** The art of judging a person's character from facial features.

ple·be·ian (plĭ-bē′ən) *adj.* **1.** Common or vulgar; coarse. **2.** Characteristic of the common people. *-n.* One of the common people.

pleb·i·scite (plĕb′ĭ-sīt′, -sĭt) *n.* A direct vote by the people on a single issue or question.

pli·a·ble (plī′ə-bəl) *adj.* **1.** Easily bent; flexible. **2.** Adaptable. **3.** Easily influenced. **-pli′a·bly,** *adv.*

pos·tu·late (pŏs′chə-lāt) *v.* **-lat·ed, -lat·ing.** To assume as true without proof. *-n.* Something assumed to be true. **-pos′tu·la′tion,** *n.*

prate (prāt) *v.* **prat·ed, prat·ing.** To talk idly and sometimes foolishly at length; chatter.

prat·tle (prăt′l) *v.* **-tled, -tling.** To chatter, talk, or babble idly, often in a meaningless or childish way. *-n.* Foolish or childish talk.

pre·clude (prĭ-klood′) *v.* **-clud·ed, -clud·ing.** To make impossible; prevent. **-pre·clu′sion,** *n.*

pre·cog·ni·tion (prē′kŏg-nĭsh′ən) *n.* Knowledge of a future event, especially by extrasensory perception.

pred·a·to·ry (prĕd′ə-tôr′ē, -tōr′ē) *adj.* **1.** Living by preying on other animals. **2.** Given to victimizing others for one's own gain. **-pred′a·tor,** *n.*

pred·i·cate (prĕd′ĭ-kāt′) *v.* **-cat·ed, -cat·ing. 1.** To base (an action, statement, etc.). **2.** To affirm as a quality or attribute of something.

pre·pense (prĭ-pĕns′) *adj.* Planned in advance; premeditated. **-pre·pense′ly,** *adv.*

pre·pos·ses·sing (prē′pə-zĕs′ĭng) *adj.* Impressing favorably; pleasing. **-pre′pos·sess′ing·ly,** *adv.*

pre·rog·a·tive (prĭ-rŏg′ə-tĭv) *n.* an exclusive right or privilege belonging to a particular person or group.

pres·age (prĕs′ĭj, prĭ-sāj′) *v.* **-saged, -sag·ing. 1.** To warn of in advance. **2.** To have a feeling beforehand. **3.** To predict. *-n.* An omen.

pre·sci·ent (prē′shē-ənt, -shənt, prĕsh′ē-ənt, prĕsh′ənt,) *adj.* Having knowledge of actions or events before they occur. **-pre′sci·ent·ly,** *adv.*

pre·scrip·tive (prĭ-skrĭp′tiv) *adj.* **1.** Set down by established custom or long use. **2.** Giving or making laws, rules, etc. **-pre·scrip′tive·ly,** *adv.*

pre·sen·ti·ment (prĭ-zĕn′tə-mənt) *n.* A feeling or sense that something is about to happen.

pre·vail (prĭ-vāl′) *v.* **1.** To triumph. **2.** To be widespread or in common use.

pre·var·i·ca·tion (prĭ-văr′ĭ-kā′shən) *n.* An evasion of the truth; a lie.

pri·mal (prī′məl) *adj.* **1.** First; original; primitive. **2.** Of first importance.

pro·fi·cient (prə-fish′ənt) *adj.* Highly competent; skilled; adept. **-pro·fi′cient·ly,** *adv.* **-pro·fi′cien·cy,** *n.*

pro·gen·i·tor (prō-jĕn′ĭ-tər) *n.* **1.** An ancestor. **2.** Originator.

prog·no·sis (prŏg-nō′sĭs) *n., pl.* **-ses** (-sez). **1.** A prediction of the probable course of a disease. **2.** A prediction or forecast.

prog·nos·ti·cate (prŏg-nŏs′tĭ-kāt) *v.* **-cat·ed, -cat·ing.** To predict or foretell on the basis of present indications.

pro·lif·ic (prə-lĭf′ĭk) *adj.* **1.** Producing abundant creative or artistic works; highly productive. **2.** Producing many offspring or fruit. **-pro·lif′ic·al·ly,** *adv.*

pro·lix·i·ty (prō-lĭk′sĭ-tē) *n.* Wordiness; long-windedness.

pro·pen·si·ty (prə-pĕn′sĭ-tē) *n., pl.* **-ties.** A natural inclination or tendency.

pro·pi·ti·ate (prō-pĭsh′ē-āt) *v.* **-at·ed, -at·ing.** To win the goodwill of; appease; satisfy.

pro·po·nent (prə-pō′nənt) *n.* A person who supports or favors something; an advocate.

pro·rogue (prə-rōg′) *v.* **-rogued, -rogu·ing. 1.** To delay; postpone. **2.** To discontinue a session of (a governing body).

pro·to·type (prō′tə-tīp) *n.* The original type, form, or model on which something is based.

pro·vin·cial (prə-vĭn′shəl) *adj.* Unsophisticated; rustic. **-pro·vin′cial·ly,** *adv.*

pseu·do·nym (sōōd′n-ĭm′) *n.* A false name, especially a pen name.

Q

quid pro quo (**kwĭd′**prō kwō′) *n., pl.* **quid pro quos** or **quids pro quo.** Something exchanged for something else.

qui·es·cent (kwē-**ĕs′**ənt, kwī-) *adj.* Being at rest; quiet; still; inactive. **-qui·es′cence,** *n.* **-qui·es′cent·ly,** *adv.*

quin·tes·sence (kwĭn-**tĕs′**əns) *n.* The purest essence of a thing. **2.** The closest-to-perfect or typical example of something.

R

rac·on·teur (rak′-ŏn-**tûr′**) *n.* A person skilled at telling stories or anecdotes.

rail·ler·y (**rā′**lə-rē) *n., pl.* **-ies.** Light, good-humored teasing; banter.

rap·proche·ment (rä′prôsh-**män′**) *n.* The establishment or renewal of harmony or friendly relations; reconciliation.

rec·on·dite (**rĕk′**ən-dīt′, rĭ-**kŏn′**dīt′) *adj.* Abstruse; difficult to understand. **-rec′on·dite′ly,** *adv.*

rec·re·ant (**rĕk′**re-ənt) *adj.* **1.** Cowardly. **2.** Disloyal or unfaithful. *-n.* **1.** A coward. **2.** A disloyal or unfaithful person.

re·crim·i·nate (rĭ-**krĭm′**ə-nāt′) *v.* **-nat·ed, -nat·ing.** To answer an accusation by accusing in return. **-re·crim′i·na·tion,** *n.*

red·o·lent (**rĕd′**əl-ənt) *adj.* **1.** Having a pleasant odor; sweet-smelling; fragrant. **2.** Suggestive; reminiscent. **-red′o·lent·ly,** *adv.*

re·gress (rĭ-**grĕs′**) *v.* **1.** To revert to an earlier or less developed state. **2.** Move backward.

re·in·force (rē′ĭn-**fôrs′**, -fôrs′) *v.* **-forced, -forc·ing.** To make stronger; strengthen.

rel·a·tive·ly (**rĕl′**ə-tĭv-lē) *adv.* In comparison with something else.

rep·li·cate (**rĕp′**lĭ-kāt′) *v.* **-cat·ed, cat·ing.** To duplicate, reproduce, repeat, or copy exactly. **-rep′li·ca′tion,** *n.*

re·proach (rĭ-**prōch′**) *v.* To express disappointment in or disapproval of someone. *-n* **1.** Blame. **2.** The act of reproaching.

re·proof (rĭ-**proof′**) *n.* Criticism; disapproval.

re·put·ed (rĭ-**pyoo′**tĭd) *adj.* Generally supposed or considered to be such; supposed. **-re·put′ed·ly,** *adv.*

re·sent·ment (rĭ-**zĕnt′**mənt) *n.* Feeling of ill will as a result of a real or imagined grievance.

res·pite (**rĕs′**pĭt) *n.* A brief interval or temporary pause or rest; pause. *-v.* To delay; postpone.

ret·ro·gres·sion (rĕt′rə-**grĕsh′**ən) *n.* The act or process of returning to a worse or less advanced stage. **-ret′ro·gres′sive,** *adj.*

rev·er·ence (**rĕv′**ər-əns) *n.* **1.** A feeling of deep respect, honor, and love. **2.** An act showing respect. **-rev′er·ent,** *adj.* **-rev′er·ent·ly,** *adv.*

ris·i·ble (**rĭz′**ə-bəl) *adj.* Causing laughter; laughable; funny. **-ris′i·bly,** *adv.*

rive (rīv) *v.* **-rived, -riv·en** (**rĭv′**ən). 1. To tear apart. **2.** To break or split.

ro·man·tic (rō-**măn′**tĭk) *adj.* Imaginative but not practical or real; idealized. **-ro·man′ti·cal·ly,** *adv.*

ru·mi·nate (**roo′**mə-nāt′) *v.* **-nat·ed, -nat·ing.** To think deeply; reflect; meditate; ponder. **-ru′mi·na′tive,** *adj.* **-ru′mi·na′tive·ly,** *adv.*

rus·tic (**rŭs′**tĭk) *adj.* **1.** Characteristic of country life or country people; rural. **2.** Unsophisticated; simple; plain. **-rus′tic·al·ly,** *adv.*

S

sac·ro·sanct (**săk′**rō-săngkt′) *adj.* Regarded as sacred and inviolable. **-sac′ro·sanc′ti·ty,** *n.*

sa·ga·cious (sə-**gā′**shəs) *adj.* Showing perception, good judgment, and farsightedness; shrewd; wise. **-sa·ga′cious·ly,** *adv.*

sa·li·ent (**sā′**lē-ənt, **săl′**yənt) *adj.* Most noticeable or conspicuous; prominent. **-sa′li·ent·ly,** *adv.*

sal·vo (**săl′**vō) *n., pl.* **-vos** or **-voes. 1.** A sudden outburst. **2.** A verbal or written attack. **3.** A firing of a number of firearms at the same time.

sanc·ti·mo·ni·ous (săngk′tə-**mō′**nē-əs) *adj.* Pretending to be very religious, pious, or righteous. **-sanc′ti·mo′ni·ous·ly,** *adv.*

san·guine (**săng′**gwĭn) *adj.* Cheerful; optimistic; confident; hopeful. **-san′guine·ly,** *adv.*

scin·til·la (sĭn-**tĭl′**ə) *n.* A very small amount; trace.

scur·ri·lous (**skûr′**ə-ləs, skŭr-) *adj.* Indecent; coarse; vulgar; foul-mouthed; abusive. **-scur′ri·lous·ly,** *adv.*

sed·u·lous (**sĕj′**ə-ləs) *adj.* Diligent and hard-working; persistent. **-sed′u·lous·ly,** *adv.*

sen·si·bil·i·ty (sĕn′sə-**bĭl′**ĭ-tē) *n.* The ability to feel, perceive, or respond.

sen·ten·tious (sĕn-**tĕn′**shəs) *adj.* **1.** Full of or inclined to pompous moralizing. **2.** Full of or liking to use trite phrases. **-sen·ten′tious·ly,** *adv.*

sen·ti·men·tal·i·ty (sĕn′tə-men-**tăl′**ĭ-tē) *n., pl.* **-ties.** The quality or condition of being excessively emotional.

sen·ti·nel (**sĕn′**tə-nəl) *n.* A person who watches for danger; guard.

se·ques·ter (sĭ-**kwĕs′**tər) *v.* **1.** To seclude; hide away. **2.** To set off or apart; separate.

shib·bo·leth (**shib′**ə-lĭth, -lĕth) *n.* A slogan, catchword, or phrase that is identified with a certain group.

sol·ace (**sŏl′**ĭs) *n.* **1.** Comfort in sorrow, grief, loneliness, etc. **2.** A person or thing that gives such comfort.

som·no·lence (**sŏm′**nə-ləns) *n.* Sleepiness; drowsiness. **-som′no·lent,** *adj.* **-som′no·lent·ly,** *adv.*

sop·o·rif·ic (sŏp′ə-**rĭf′**ĭk, sō′pə-) *adj.* Causing or tending to cause sleep. *-n.* Something that causes sleep.

sor·did (**sôr′**dĭd) *adj.* **1.** Dirty; filthy; foul. **2.** Wretched; squalid. **3.** Morally base; mean. **-sor′did·ly,** *adv.*

spare (spâr) *adj.* **spar·er, spar·est. 1.** Not excessive or lavish. **2.** Extra. **3.** Lean; thin.

spec·ter (**spĕk′**tər) *n.* **1.** A ghost. **2.** A haunting image.

spec·trum (**spĕk′**trəm) *n., pl.* **-tra** (-trə) or **-trums. 1.** A band of colors into which light is separated as it passes through a prism. **2.** A broad range.

sti·pend (**stī′**pĕnd, -pənd) *n.* A regular fixed payment or allowance, such as a salary.

stri·ate (strī′āt) *v.* **-at·ed, -at·ing.** To mark with narrow grooves or streaks that are usually parallel. **-stri·a′tion,** *n.*

stric·ture (strĭk′chər) *n.* **1.** Restriction; limitation. **2.** An adverse criticism.

stul·ti·fy (stŭl′tə-fī′) *v.* **-fied, -fy·ing, -fies. 1.** To make useless or weak. **2.** To cause to seem stupid. **3.** To have an inhibiting effect on.

sub·ro·gate (sŭb′rō-gāt′) *v.* **-gat·ed, -gat·ing.** To substitute one person or thing for another.

sub·ter·fuge (sŭb′tər-fyo͞oj) *n.* A trick, device, or plan used to evade, deceive, or hide.

suf·fice (sə-fīs′) *v.* **-ficed, -fic·ing.** To be enough or adequate to meet or satisfy the needs or requirements of; be sufficient.

sun·dry (sŭn′drē) *adj.* Various.

su·per·cil·i·ous (so͞o′pər-sĭl′ē-əs) *adj.* Showing excessive pride; haughty; disdainful. **su′per·cil′i·ous·ly,** *adv.*

sup·ple (sŭp′əl) *adj.* **-pler, -plest. 1.** Easily bent; pliant. **2.** Flexible. **-sup′ple·ness,** *n.*

sur·feit (sûr′fĭt) *n.* **1.** An excessive amount. **2.** Overindulgence. *-v.* To feed or supply to excess.

sur·ly (sûr′lē) *adj.* **-li·er, -li·est.** Sullenly rude; bad-tempered; uncivil. **-sur′li·ness,** *n.*

sur·ro·gate (sûr′ə-gĭt, -gāt′, sŭr′-) *n.* One that takes the place of another; a substitute. *-adj.* Substitute. *-v.* To put in the place of another.

svelte (svĕlt) *adj.* **svelt·er, svelt·est.** Slender and graceful.

syc·o·phant (sĭk′ə-fənt, sī′kə-) *n.* A person who flatters influential or wealthy people in order to gain favor or influence. **-syc′o·phan′tic,** *adj.*

T

tac·it (tăs′ĭt) *adj.* **1.** Not spoken. **2.** Not openly expressed but implied or understood.

tac·i·turn (tăs′ĭ-tûrn) *adj.* Not talkative; uncommunicative; silent. **-tac′i·turn·ly,** *adv.*

ti·rade (tī′rād, tī′rād′) *n.* A long, angry speech.

trans·mute (trăns-myo͞ot′, trănz-) *v.* **-mut·ed, -mut·ing.** To change from one form, substance, species, or quality into another. **-trans′mu·ta′tion,** *n.*

trench·ant (trĕn′chənt) *adj.* **1.** Sharp; cutting; incisive. **2.** Forceful; effective. **-trench′an·cy,** *n.*

truc·u·lent (trŭk′yə-lənt) *adj.* **1.** Fierce, savage, or ferocious. **2.** Rude, harsh, or scathing. **3.** Belligerent; disposed to fight. **-truc′u·lent·ly,** *adv.*

U-V-W

un·con·scion·a·ble (ŭn-kŏn′shə-nə-bəl) *adj.* **1.** Not guided or restrained by conscience; unscrupulous. **2.** Shockingly unfair or unjust. **-un·con′scion·a·bly,** *adv.*

un·du·late (ŭn′jə-lāt, ŭn′dyə-,-də-) *v.* **-lat·ed, -lat·ing. 1.** To move in waves. **2.** To have a wavy appearance. *-adj.* Having a wavy form. **-un·du·la′tion,** *n.*

ven·det·ta (vĕn-dĕt′ə) *n.* A bitter feud or quarrel.

ver·tex (vûr′tĕks′) *n., pl.* **-tex·es** or **-ti·ces** (-tĭ-sēz). The highest point; top; apex.

ver·tig·i·nous (vər-tĭj′ə-nəs) *adj.* **1.** Revolving; rotating; whirling. **2.** Dizzy. **-ver·tig′i·nous·ly,** *adv.*

ver·ti·go (vûr′tĭ-gō′) *n.*, *pl.* **-goes** or **-gos.** The sensation of dizziness.

ves·tige (vĕs′tĭj) *n.* A visible sign, trace, or evidence, especially of something that no longer exists.

vis·cer·al (vĭs′ər-əl) *adj.* 1. Of, relating to, or affecting the internal organs of the body. 2. Profound; deep.

vi·ti·a·tion (vĭsh′ē-ā′shən) *n.* 1. The state of being corrupted or invalidated. 2. The act of corrupting or invalidating. **-vi′ti·ate,** *v.*

vi·tu·per·a·tive (vī-tōō′pər-ə-tĭv, -tyōō-, -pə-rā′-, vĭ-) *adj.* Using, containing, or characterized by harsh, abusive, or bitter language. **-vi·tu′per·a′tion,** *n.*

vor·tex (vôr′tĕks) *n.*, *pl.* **-tex·es** or **-ti·ces** (-tĭ-sēz′). A whirling mass, especially water or air, that sucks nearby things into its center; whirlpool.

whim·si·cal (hwĭm′zĭ-kəl, wĭm′-) *adj.* 1. Characterized by an odd or imaginative notion; fanciful. 2. Unpredictable. **-whim′si·cal·ly,** *adv.*

Standardized Test Practice

In lessons 1 to 36, you have concentrated on building vocabulary, a skill that is an important aid in reading comprehension. However, the competent reader must master a variety of other skills. These include the following:

- **Identifying main and subordinate ideas**—deciding what the most important idea in the selection is and what items support that idea

Examples:

| Main idea | Marcel Marceau is the master of mime, the wordless theater. |
| Subordinate ideas | Marceau admired Charlie Chaplin, Buster Keaton, and the Marx Brothers, all of whom used mime in their performances. Marceau tells most of his stories through Bip the clown, a character he created. Marceau's aim is to make his audiences see, feel, and hear the invisible. |

- **Deciding on an appropriate title**—choosing a title that is closely related to the main idea of a selection

- **Drawing inferences**—coming to a conclusion that is not directly stated but is based on information given

Example:

If a woman is clasping her purse tightly and looking around her, you can infer that she is afraid her purse will be stolen.

- **Locating details**—scanning a selection to find the answer to a specific question

The following pages will give you a chance to practice the skills you use when you read. The questions they contain are the kinds of questions you will be asked to answer on a standardized test.

The reading selections include passages from science and social studies texts as well as informative essays and short narratives.

Reread "William Tell: Man or Myth?" on page 15 and answer the following questions. Circle the letter that precedes the BEST answer to each question.

1. What ideal does William Tell symbolize?

   A. the importance of good sportsmanship

   B. the spirit of cooperation

   C. the passion for freedom

   D. the right to bear arms

2. Which of the following statements is most accurate?

   A. William Tell lived during the latter part of the sixteenth century.

   B. Stories of William Tell's deeds have been authenticated by modern historians.

   C. William Tell was honored for rescuing the governor and his men from a violent storm on Lake Lucerne.

   D. William Tell was punished for insubordination by being made to shoot an arrow through an apple resting on his son's head.

3. What ruling group controlled Switzerland in the thirteenth century?

   A. Russian tsars

   B. German emperors

   C. the Hapsburgs of Austria

   D. the royal Tudor family of England

4. Which of these heroic figures does William Tell most closely resemble?

   A. Robin Hood

   B. Paul Bunyan

   C. Johnny Appleseed

   D. Christopher Columbus

5. Which of the following statements is true about a country with an *egalitarian* government?

   A. It is ruled by a king.

   B. All of its citizens have equal rights.

   C. The legislature consists of two houses.

   D. Laws must be approved by rulers before they are enforced.

Reread the selection "Three Laws That Must Be Obeyed" on page 71 and answer the following questions. Circle the letter that precedes the BEST answer to each question.

1. Where was Sir Isaac Newton when he formulated his three laws of motion?

   A. in a dormitory at Cambridge University

   B. in a well-equipped laboratory

   C. at his mother's farm

   D. under an apple tree

2. What is the main idea of the selection on page 71?

   A. Laws were instituted for the benefit of all citizens.

   B. Newton's Laws of Motion are illustrated in many everyday situations.

   C. Citizens can choose whether they will obey Newton's Laws of Motion.

   D. Sir Isaac Newton credited his scientific contributions to the work of scientists who preceded him.

3. How can Newton's First Law of Motion be restated?

   A. The farther an object moves, the slower its speed.

   B. For every action there is an equal and opposite reaction.

   C. Objects in motion remain in motion unless they are acted on by an outside force.

   D. If a heavy object and a light object are pushed with the same force, the heavy object will move farther.

4. Which item might best be described as a *behemoth?*

   A. a ten-speed racing bicycle

   B. a birch bark canoe

   C. a Segway scooter

   D. a monster truck

5. According to the selection, at what period of his life did Newton formulate the laws of motion?

   A. during a break in his studies at Cambridge University

   B. when he became well-known in scientific circles

   C. near the end of his illustrious scientific career

   D. information not provided in the selection

Reread the selection "Maya Lin's Architecture of Remembrance" on page 85 and answer the following questions. Circle the letter that precedes the BEST answer to each question.

1. What would be another appropriate title for this selection?

    A. The Life of Maya Lin

    B. Teaching with Architecture

    C. A Chinese American Architect

    D. Maya Lin's Famous Memorials

2. What is the purpose of Maya Lin's public memorials?

    A. to teach historical lessons

    B. to move viewers to sadness

    C. to allow viewers to make their own interpretations

    D. to demonstrate the architect's understanding of events

3. Which of the following can be inferred from the selection?

    A. Maya Lin designs both public and private sculptures.

    B. Maya Lin devotes her talents to designing public memorials.

    C. Public sculpture is not intended to evoke an emotional response.

    D. Maya Lin's plans for the Vietnam Wall won widespread approval from veterans.

4. What group proved that it was favorably impressed by Lin's architectural skill?

    A. the Daughters of the American Revolution

    B. the Southern Poverty Law Center

    C. the Veterans of Foreign Wars

    D. the House of Representatives

5. What kind of situation is an *imbroglio?*

    A. a formal planning session

    B. a complicated disagreement

    C. a long, drawn-out panel discussion

    D. a meeting with government officials

Read the selection "Teetering between Terror and Ecstasy" on page 141 and answer the following questions. Circle the letter that precedes the BEST answer to each question.

1. Who originated the idea of a roller coaster?

    A. a Russian empress

    B. a Coney Island entrepreneur

    C. the Greek philosopher Aristotle

    D. a scientist studying weightlessness

2. What makes it possible for today's roller coasters to have extremely steep inclines and sharp turns?

    A. the combined experience of many years

    B. the assistance of engineering experts

    C. computer-simulated models

    D. more-daring riders

3. Why have roller coasters maintained their popularity over the years?

    A. They are an inexpensive amusement.

    B. It takes nerve, not skill, to ride a roller coaster.

    C. There have never been any accidents involving roller coasters.

    D. Riding a roller coaster combines fun and fear, happiness and horror.

4. On which of these occasions might you experience a *visceral* feeling?

    A. You are admiring a collection of art masterpieces.

    B. On a camping trip, a bear starts to destroy your tent during the night.

    C. You learn that you have been accepted at the college of your choice.

    D. You have won a trip to the Hawaiian Islands, the first prize in an essay contest.

5. After roller coaster cars have been pulled up an incline, what causes the cars to drop?

    A. A hidden pulley draws the cars downward.

    B. Newton's Third Law of Motion takes effect.

    C. Potential energy is converted into kinetic energy.

    D. The riders in the cars shift their weight downward.

Ramses the Great

by Rick Gore, *National Geographic,* April 1, 1991

In the year 1279 B.C. the Sphinx, that great man-animal monument that stands near the ancient Egyptian capital of Memphis, was already more than a thousand years old. A young warrior strides between its paws. He is dressed in regal garb, a ceremonial wig concealing his close-cropped hair.

On a colossal statue that scholars now suspect stood between the paws, he orders workers to chisel in his throne name, User-maat-re—Strong-in-truth-is-Re. And beside that inscription he commands them to carve his personal name, Ramesse—or, to us, Ramses the Great.

He will reign more than 60 years, sire at least 90 children, bring his empire prosperity and peace, build more colossal structures and have his name carved on more stone surfaces than any other pharaoh. He will be linked also with the Exodus of the Hebrews.

Our perception of Ramses has long been colored by the English poet Percy Bysshe Shelley. He wrote his famous sonnet "Ozymandias" after a magnificent bust of Ramses, found near a shattered colossus at the pharaoh's funerary temple in Thebes, was shipped with great fanfare to the British Museum in 1817. Shelley imagined Ramses as a symbol of tyranny and unbridled egotism.

But there must have been another side. At the British Museum, I had visited the Ramses bust with Egyptologist Kenneth Kitchen of the University of Liverpool. Kitchen has spent the past 22 years translating and studying the 2,000 pages of hieroglyphs that relate to Ramses. He is the world's leading authority on the man. We looked up at the bust.

"See, Shelley got it wrong," said Kitchen. "Our man never sneers. Look at his lips. He smiles. Gently. It's a lovely poem, but I'm afraid it's pure Shelley."

Kitchen's work and new archaeological interpretations are indeed helping us to see beyond the cruel and romantic vision of Ramses. As this scholarship enriches our knowledge of ancient Egypt, it is rounding out a more human portrait of this towering figure. Who was the man behind the great stone mask? That is the question that pulled me to Egypt.

Circle the letter that precedes the BEST answer to each of the following questions.

1. With which of the following statements would the author most likely agree?

    A. Ramses the Great was a tyrant and an unbridled egotist.

    B. Ramses the Great is a fascinating but mysterious historical figure.

    C. The identity of the man behind the great stone mask still is not known.

    D. Kenneth Kitchen is the most knowledgeable authority on Egyptian history.

2. According to the passage, what was Ramses the Great's throne name?

    A. Sphinx

    B. Memphis

    C. Ozymandias

    D. User-maat-re

3. What is the purpose of the third paragraph of the passage?

    A. To describe further the statue beneath the Sphinx

    B. To introduce the discussion of the English poet Percy Bysshe Shelley's "Ozymandias"

    C. To list some of the accomplishments of Ramses the Great

    D. To explain why Ramses the Great is mentioned in the Bible

4. According to the passage, what is a sphinx?

    A. Part animal and part human

    B. The ruler of ancient Egypt

    C. A young Egyptian warrior

    D. A Hebrew prophet

5. Why does the author mention Shelley's poem?

    A. To demonstrate the effect that poems have on great rulers

    B. To suggest why people believe that Ramses the Great was a tyrant

    C. To explain how the Egyptologist Kitchen conducted his study

    D. To prove that "Ozymandias" was based on a close study of hieroglyphs

6. According to the passage, where was Ramses the Great buried?

    A. Thebes

    B. Memphis

    C. Liverpool

    D. The British Museum

7. Read the following passage from the article:

> **"See, Shelley got it wrong," said Kitchen. "Our man never sneers. Look at his lips. He smiles. Gently. It's a lovely poem, but I'm afraid it's pure Shelley."**

Why does Kitchen say "Our man never sneers"?

A. To confirm that Ramses really was a terrible tyrant

B. To disprove Shelley's image of Ramses as an egotist

C. To give people a cruel and romantic vision of Ramses

D. To demonstrate a typical characteristic of ancient statues

8. Which of the following can be inferred from information in the passage?

A. Ramses was ninety years old when he died.

B. Shelley's poem "Ozymandias" was written in 1817.

C. The Sphinx is now more than four thousand years old.

D. Liverpool is the world's best center of Egyptian studies.

from The Real Life of Sebastian Knight

by Vladimir Nabokov

In November of 1918 my mother resolved to flee with [my brother] Sebastian and myself from the dangers of Russia. Revolution was in full swing; frontiers were closed. She got in touch with a man who had made smuggling refugees across the border his profession, and it was settled that for a certain fee, one half of which was paid in advance, he would get us to Finland. We were to leave the train just before the frontier, at a place we could lawfully reach, and then cross over by secret paths, doubly, trebly secret owing to the heavy snowfalls in that silent region. At the starting-point of our train journey, we found ourselves, my mother and I, waiting for Sebastian, who, with the heroic help of Captain Belov, was trundling the luggage from house to station. The train was scheduled to start at 8:40 A.M. Half past and still no Sebastian. Our guide was already in the train and sat quietly reading a newspaper; he had warned my mother that in no circumstance should she talk to him in public, and as the time passed and the train was preparing to leave, a nightmare feeling of numb panic began to come over us. We knew that the man, in accordance with the traditions of his profession, would never renew a performance that had misfired at the outset. We knew too that we could not again afford the expenses of flight. The minutes passed and I felt something gurgling desperately in the pit of my stomach. The thought that in a minute or two the train would move off and that we should have to return to a dark cold attic (our house had been nationalised some months ago) was utterly disastrous. On our way to the station we had passed Sebastian and Belov pushing the heavily burdened wheelbarrow through the crunching snow. This picture now stood motionless before my eyes (I was a boy of thirteen and very imaginative) as a charmed thing doomed to its paralysed eternity. My mother, her hands in her sleeves and a wisp of grey hair emerging from beneath her woolen kerchief, walked to and fro, trying to catch the eye of our guide every time she passed by his window. Eight forty-five, eight-fifty . . . The train was late in starting, but at last the whistle blew, a rush of warm white smoke raced its shadow across the brown snow on the platform, and at the same time Sebastian appeared running, the earflaps of his fur cap flying in the wind. The three of us scrambled into the moving train.

Circle the letter that precedes the BEST answer to each of the following questions.

1. What family difficulty does the story describe?

   A. opposing the Russian Revolution

   B. moving the family's belongings to a new house

   C. finding the family's lost child, Sebastian, in time

   D. convincing a guide to talk to family members on the train

2. Why does Sebastian's family want to leave Russia?

   A. The weather there is too cold for them.

   B. The Revolution has made living there dangerous.

   C. The police have been looking for Sebastian's mother.

   D. The family wants to find relatives in another country.

3. Read the following excerpt from the passage:

   . . . as the time passed and the train was preparing to leave, a nightmare feeling of numb panic began to come over us.

   What is the main cause of the narrator and his mother's panic?

   A. They know that they cannot pay the guide his fee.

   B. They think that Sebastian has joined the Revolution.

   C. They think that Captain Belov has stolen their luggage.

   D. They are afraid that Sebastian will not arrive in time and the train will leave without them.

4. During most of the story, where are the narrator and his mother waiting for Sebastian?

   A. on the platform of a train station

   B. outside their new attic apartment

   C. at the border of Russia and Finland

   D. inside a train compartment with their guide

5. Read the following sentence from the passage:

   We were to leave the train just before the frontier, at a place we could lawfully reach, and then cross over by secret paths, doubly, trebly secret owing to the heavy snowfalls in that silent region.

   Which word or phrase best defines the meaning of the word *trebly?*

   A. shivering   C. three times

   B. carefully hidden   D. completely silent

6. What word best describes the narrator's mood at the time the story takes place?

    A. anxious

    B. relaxed

    C. romantic

    D. objective

7. Why will the family members have to return to a dark cold attic if they do not get on the train?

    A. They can no longer live with Captain Belov.

    B. The winter in Finland has been extremely snowy.

    C. Their house has been confiscated by the government.

    D. Sebastian has sold their belongings to pay for the trip.

8. Read the following excerpt from the passage:

    We knew that the man, in accordance with the traditions of his profession, would never renew a performance that had misfired at the outset. We knew too that we could not again afford the expenses of flight.

    What is the main purpose of these sentences?

    A. to explain why the family cannot talk to the smuggler on the train

    B. to demonstrate the reason for Sebastian's late arrival at the station

    C. to point out that this is the family's only chance of getting out of Russia

    D. to convince the reader that the family will be killed if members do not reach Finland

9. Why does the narrator point out that he was very imaginative at the age of thirteen?

    A. It demonstrates that he is having a dream while riding on the train.

    B. It suggests that the creativity of a writer was evident early in his life.

    C. It shows that he has the strength to help his family escape from Russia.

    D. It explains why he pictures Sebastian pushing a wheelbarrow through the snow.

10. What occurrence helps the family catch the train before it leaves?

    A. The train leaves the station at least ten minutes late.

    B. Sebastian gets help bringing the baggage to the station.

    C. The guide allows the family to board the train without Sebastian.

    D. The narrator bribes the conductor to let the family cross into Finland.

Read the following selection and answer the questions that follow.

Stolen Whitman Papers Surface after 50 Years

by David Streitfield and Elizabeth Kastor, *Washington Post,* February 18, 1995

Four long-lost notebooks by Walt Whitman, stolen from the Library of Congress a half-century ago, have been recovered, Sotheby's auction house said yesterday. Found by a man among his father's papers, the notebooks will be returned to the library.

"This is definitely the most important literary material we could have hoped to recover of anything known in American literature," said David Wigdor, assistant chief of the library's manuscript division.

Six Whitman notebooks are still missing. The 10 stolen volumes were part of a total of 24 donated to the library in 1924 by Thomas B. Harned.

The man who brought the notebooks to Sotheby's in New York has chosen to remain anonymous. He told the auction house that his father had received the material as a gift about 30 years ago. The FBI, which investigated the case in the '40s, is once again pursuing it, according to the Library of Congress.

If the notebooks were not stolen material, they would have brought a presale estimate of $350,000 to $500,000, said Selby Kiffer, a vice president in Sotheby's books and manuscripts department.

The man who approached Sotheby's with the documents was "stunned" when he was told what he had, Kiffer said. "When he realized that he wouldn't be selling them he was stunned and I think slightly depressed, as I think anyone would be. On the other hand, he was incredibly cooperative. . . . He feels he has done his part, and his role is ended." No money is changing hands in the return of the papers.

The rediscovered notebooks include essays on perception and the human senses, names and addresses of friends, and drafts of Civil War poems. Whitman also kept notes about some of the wounded soldiers he tended in Washington [D.C.] in 1862. "bed 15— wants an orange . . . bed 59 wants some liquorice . . . 27 wants some figs and a book," he wrote. Next to some of these jottings were crosses, suggesting the nameless subjects had died.

Circle the letter that precedes the BEST answer to each of the following questions.

1. Which word best describes the tone adopted by the author of the article?

   A. amused   C. outraged

   B. stunned   D. objective

2. What is the most likely reason that the man who returned the notebook was "slightly depressed"?

   A. He suddenly realized that his father had been a criminal all his life.

   B. He was concerned about the FBI's pressing charges against his family.

   C. He had believed he was going to make a lot of money selling the notebooks.

   D. He owed half a million dollars to the man who gave his father the notebooks.

3. Which of the following is true according to the article?

   A. Six of the ten stolen notebooks are still missing.

   B. Sotheby's plans to sell the notebooks to the FBI.

   C. Walt Whitman first became a famous poet during the Civil War.

   D. The Library of Congress has none of Walt Whitman's notebooks.

4. Why were the stolen notebooks first returned to Sotheby's and not to the Library of Congress?

   A. The notebooks were insured for up to $500,000 by Sotheby's.

   B. Sotheby's is the owner of the entire collection of 24 notebooks.

   C. The man who had the notebooks wanted to sell them in an auction.

   D. The Library of Congress had bought the notebooks from Sotheby's.

5. Read the following sentence from the article:

   If the notebooks were not stolen material, they would have brought a presale estimate of $350,000 to $500,000, said Selby Kiffer, a vice president in Sotheby's books and manuscripts department.

   What was the author's purpose in mentioning the presale estimate?

   A. to point out how valuable the notebooks are

   B. to explain why the FBI was still interested in the case

   C. to show how much the Library of Congress originally paid for the notebooks

   D. to prove that the man's father could have received the notebooks only as a gift

Read the following selection and then follow the directions.

The Righting Reflex

from *The Natural History of Cats* by Claire Necker

1   We all know that the cat is usually unhurt when it falls from a height because it lands on its feet. The Persians have a saying that Ali [revered as the successor to the prophet Muhammed] passed his hand along its back one day to make this possible. How it is accomplished is another matter. The physiology and mechanics of this seemingly simple act are intricate and involved and not yet completely understood. It is a superb example of pure reflex; if the cat had to think about what to do next as it dropped through space, it would never survive its first fall.

2   Cats need this safeguard, and they seem to rely on it far too much. Agile and quick-witted though they are, they fall from windows, trees, and other heights with predictable regularity and for no apparent reason other than carelessness or excitement. While in precarious positions, they overestimate their reaching capacity in their eagerness to grasp something, and they insist on rolling in happy abandon on the brink of small and great drops. They do any number of thoughtless things such as these, which are entirely inconsistent with their cautious nature and which frequently result in a fall. Scratches on cat owners' thighs and furniture, the result of last-minute attempts on the cat's part to save itself, are ample evidence of their folly. Yet on landing from a fall, a cat will often go back to its original location to continue from where it was interrupted unless, realizing that its mistake has been observed, it stalks off with as much dignity as it can summon. Woe to those who laugh at it under these circumstances.

3   According to Moncrif in his "Les Chats," a description of the cat's righting reflex was published in the *Memoires de l'Académie des Sciences* in 1700. Almost 200 years later, in 1894, the academy published another article on the subject, this time an analysis of photographs that show a cat performing the act. Numerous articles, both popular and scientific, have subsequently been published in English.

4   Through physiological experimentation, it is now known that the labyrinth or inner ear plays the greater part in a cat's feet-first landing. It is already functional in the 54-day-old cat fetus, that is, in a fetus 6 days before birth. The *body*-righting reflex is present almost a week earlier, on the 49th day. This part of the reflex is initiated by the proprioceptive impulses of the muscles and the exteroceptive impulses of the skin. (*Proprioceptive* means receiving stimulations within the tissues of the *body*. Besides being present in the labyrinth, proprioceptors are located throughout the body, principally in muscles and tendons. They are sensory nerve terminals which give an animal information concerning the movement and positions of its body. *Exteroceptors* are those nerve terminals which give information received from the external environment.)

5 The righting reflex is therefore triggered by such signals as (1) the cat's feet losing contact with something solid, that is, losing their normal tactile sensation, (2) the eyes registering an abnormal body position through external stimuli, (3) the muscles, etc., registering the same through internal stimuli, and (4) the ear registering an upset equilibrium.

6 Skin, eyes, ears, muscle proprioceptors—at least four senses act together to produce a reflex act far too rapid for the eye to register. Blindness or inner ear injury do not prevent a perfect landing unless both handicaps exist together. The cat will then land "any which way," as we do when we fall. Even figuratively speaking, very few humans manage to land feet first; the proverb "No matter what happens he always lands on his feet" indicates the relative rarity of such an occurrence.

7 Other vertebrates—like squirrels, monkeys, frogs, dogs, and rabbits—do share in the righting reflex with cats but not to as great a degree. Cats are masters in the art.

Circle the letter that precedes the BEST answer to each of the following questions.

1. The author's main objective in this essay is to
   A. put forth fairly both sides of a scientific debate.
   B. explain just one tiny part of a complex physiological phenomenon.
   C. illustrate the gaps in what science understands about the phenomenon discussed.
   D. propose an alternative explanation for the development of the reflexes of a particular animal.

2. In paragraph 5, the word *upset* most closely means
   A. invisible.
   B. saddened.
   C. disturbed.
   D. complicated.

3. The author's comment at the end of paragraph 2, "Woe to those who laugh at it under these circumstances," is intended to
   A. draw a conclusion in regard to a previously posed question.
   B. inject some levity into a mostly scientific discussion.
   C. emphasize the seriousness of empirical observation.
   D. make a complaint about a common situation.

4. The author mentions old studies of the cat mostly in order to
   A. explain early theories regarding the reflex.
   B. contrast the French style of research with that of the English.
   C. show the degree to which early theories have been disproved.
   D. demonstrate how long scientists have been studying this reflex.

Copyright © Glencoe/McGraw-Hill, a division of The McGraw-Hill Companies, Inc.

5. The author suggests that physiological experiments with cats suggest that the "body-righting reflex" mentioned in paragraph 4 is

    A. an easily acquired behavior.

    B. probably an innate characteristic.

    C. caused by the cat's ability to land feet first.

    D. influential in causing certain muscle impulses.

6. In paragraph 5, the word *triggered* refers to

    A. a cat's leaping ability.

    B. the development of a cat's reflexes.

    C. the activation of the righting reflex.

    D. the reception of certain external signals.

7. Of the following, the statement that, if true, would most weaken the author's position (that "cats are the masters of the art" of landing on their feet—paragraph 7) is

    A. In one study, a cat with an injured ear, temporarily blinded by smoke from a fire, failed to land on his feet when it fell only two feet.

    B. Some cats in a recent study could not land on their feet at all while on a medication that affects the nervous system.

    C. Many other animals share some of the physiological characteristics that contribute to the righting reflex.

    D. New evidence shows that many animals can and do land upright just as frequently.

8. The author probably believes that our understanding of the reasons a cat is able to land on its feet

    A. is still extremely limited.

    B. has been growing for well over two hundred years.

    C. has been greatly enhanced by our knowledge of human reflexes.

    D. results primarily from society's acceptance of cats as house pets.

Word List

Word	Lesson	Word	Lesson	Word	Lesson
abeyance	23	compendium	27	equipoise	27
abrogate	3	complacent	23	eschew	32
abstruse	28	complicity	30	ethics	28
accoutrements	10	compulsion	28	exasperate	28
acronym	24	concord	23	exhort	13
ad hoc	20	conscientious	9	expatiate	29
ad infinitum	20	consensus	6	expendable	27
adjudge	17	controversy	7	explicit	30
adorn	1	conventional	4	extirpate	28
affable	23	corroborate	2	extol	2
affectation	12	coruscate	1	facetious	29
affidavit	18	credence	18	facile	12
aficionado	28	credibility	18	factitious	12
agog	22	credulous	18	fallacy	2
alacrity	11	crux	7	fastidious	10
allege	22	dally	16	fealty	18
amorphous	33	debilitate	25	feasible	12
anathema	8	deferential	5	feline	25
anonymity	24	deleterious	32	fiduciary	18
antipode	25	demur	2	filigree	1
aperture	34	denomination	24	flagrant	35
apocryphal	16	deplore	7	flamboyant	35
apologist	2	deprecate	8	flaunt	35
appendage	27	depreciate	16	flippant	34
arabesque	1	derogatory	3	forestall	32
archaic	7	devotee	34	fugacious	1
arrogate	3	diadem	36	functional	10
askew	7	diametrical	36	furtive	35
assent	6	diaphanous	36	fusillade	25
asymmetrical	19	diatribe	36	genealogy	15
austere	26	didactic	19	genteel	31
aversion	21	diffident	18	genus	15
avert	21	dilettante	26	germinal	15
axiomatic	2	disapprobation	8	glabrous	25
behemoth	16	discourse	29	glean	22
berate	17	disparage	17	Gothic	13
bestial	14	dispassionate	34	guise	4
blatant	35	disquisition	29	gyrate	31
bourgeois	26	dissent	6	halcyon	23
brevity	16	dissolution	7	harrowing	31
bromide	29	dissuade	2	heinous	14
bucolic	23	distraught	31	hiatus	32
cabal	20	duplicity	30	homonym	24
canker	14	éclat	26	hyperbolic	33
capitulate	28	edify	19	hypercritical	33
carping	5	effete	14	hypersensitive	33
caste	26	efficacy	12	hyperventilate	33
castigate	17	egalitarian	4	hypochondria	33
cause célèbre	20	egress	15	hypocrite	33
celerity	11	elite	13	hypothermia	33
chaotic	7	engender	7	hypothesis	33
chastise	8	ennui	11	ignominy	24
chide	17	entrance	22	imbroglio	19
chutzpah	20	enumerate	22	impertinent	4
circuitous	32	epidermis	36	imperturbable	23
circumvent	32	episodic	36	impetus	4
cognizant	9	epistemology	36	implicit	30
coherent	7	epitaph	36	impregnable	13
coiffure	25	epithet	36	inadvertent	21
commute	30	epitome	36	incensed	4

Word	Lesson	Word	Lesson	Word	Lesson
incise	19	perpend	27	risible	25
incontrovertible	21	persona non grata	20	rive	13
indigent	26	perverse	14	romantic	10
indolent	11	philippic	17	ruminate	2
inert	23	phlegmatic	5	rustic	10
inexorable	31	physiognomy	9	sacrosanct	1
inexplicable	30	plebian	26	sagacious	3
infallible	22	plebiscite	9	salient	35
ingress	15	pliable	23	salvo	25
insensate	6	postulate	2	sanctimonious	5
insinuation	17	prate	29	sanguine	5
insouciance	34	prattle	29	scintilla	22
insularity	13	preclude	10	scurrilous	5
interrogate	3	precognition	9	sedulous	11
intrepid	4	predatory	14	sensibility	6
intuitive	19	predicate	7	sententious	6
invective	8	prepense	27	sentimentality	6
ironic	28	prepossessing	10	sentinel	6
juggernaut	20	prerogative	3	sequester	35
kinetic	31	presage	3	shibboleth	20
languor	11	prescient	9	solace	19
lethargic	5	prescriptive	1	somnolence	11
lissome	11	presentiment	6	soporific	11
malinger	32	prevail	22	sordid	14
malversation	21	prevarication	32	spare	19
masochist	31	primal	13	specter	1
melange	22	proficient	12	spectrum	34
metonymy	24	progenitor	15	stipend	27
miscreant	18	prognosis	9	striate	19
misnomer	24	prognosticate	9	stricture	17
modest	1	prolific	12	stultify	32
morpheme	33	prolixity	29	subrogate	3
munificent	26	propensity	27	subterfuge	32
mutate	30	propitiate	34	suffice	12
mystique	13	proponent	34	sundry	13
nabob	20	prorogue	3	supercilious	17
nexus	31	prototype	10	supple	19
nomenclature	24	provincial	26	surfeit	12
nominal	24	pseudonym	24	surly	5
obeisance	4	quid pro quo	20	surrogate	3
obscure	28	quiescent	11	svelte	16
obsequious	2	quintessence	34	sycophant	26
obtrusive	35	raconteur	29	tacit	15
obverse	21	raillery	29	taciturn	15
odious	14	rapprochement	34	tirade	17
offal	14	recondite	35	transmute	30
officious	12	recreant	18	trenchant	8
omniscient	9	recriminate	8	truculent	5
pacific	23	redolent	10	unconscionable	9
palaver	22	regress	15	undulate	31
palpable	1	reinforce	16	vendetta	25
paranoid	25	relatively	16	vertex	21
paraphrase	16	replicate	30	vertiginous	21
partisan	4	reproach	8	vertigo	21
patina	10	reproof	8	vestige	35
patronizing	5	reputed	4	visceral	31
penchant	27	resentment	6	vitiation	14
pensive	27	respite	16	vituperative	8
perfidious	18	retrogression	15	vortex	21
permutation	30	reverence	13	whimsical	28